The TRIUMPH *of* REALISM
in
ELIZABETHAN DRAMA
1558-1612

by

WILLARD THORP

HASKELL HOUSE
Publishers of Scholarly Books
NEW YORK
1965

published by

HASKELL HOUSE
Publishers of Scholarly Books
30 East 10th Street • New York, N. Y. 10003

Library of Congress Catalog Card Number: 65-21093

PRINTED IN UNITED STATES OF AMERICA

FOREWORD

Apologies are out of fashion. But in the days of Queen Elizabeth no self-respecting author thought of offering a work to his patron without one. There is consequently some propriety in beginning a thesis in Elizabethan literature by apologizing for its lack of completeness; even Shakespeare asked indulgence for the "unpolished lines" of the "first heir" of his invention, the *Venus and Adonis*.

I have undertaken to do what only a grey-beard should attempt: the relating of a body of great literature to the civilization which nourished it. To do this with illuminating results one should be conversant not only with the literature itself but as well with the law, theology, social customs, and philosophy of the age—obviously an impossible achievement for a few months or a few years. And so, though I have tried to keep constantly before me the larger question of the extent to which these plays that I have been pondering may be trusted as an authentic record of the temper of Elizabethan society, I have necessarily confined my researches to one phase of the whole problem. I shall try to make clear precisely what that phase is.

The drama which was produced in the provinces, in the City of London and at the Court in the first days of Elizabeth's reign, was really medieval notwithstanding the fact that neo-classical influences had already begun to work a change on its form and content. It was often rambling in structure and its realism was still of the sort which the miracles supported, horse-play, tumbling, and the antics of rustics, tavern-brawlers, and half-witted clowns. No strongly individualized characters belonging to a higher order of society can be found in these plays. But the most pronounced feature of the early Elizabethan drama is its didacticism, now extended from the realm of theology to embrace as well politics, sociology and education. It falls like a heavy pall on the stories, grave and gay, which filtered into England and found their way to the stage. It is a part of the medieval inheritance of Renaissance England which is elsewhere exemplified in the superstition of the age, the folk-lore survivals, the love of pageantry and play, the fondness for singing and dancing. It is perhaps the strongest evidence of the fact that the concept of a Renaissance is a fiction of historians, since England had been exposed for nearly a hundred years to the paganism of the New Learning which encouraged men to question before believing what they were taught.

vii

Very different indeed is the drama which prevailed in the days immediately following the death of Elizabeth, so different in fact from that of fifty years before that the name Elizabethan applied to both seems ludicrous. Yet there was no break between. The evolution had been constant. The most evident characteristic of this new drama is its romantic nature, if by the word romantic one is allowed to mean the use of foreign stories and settings. Shakespeare only once tells a tale of contemporary England. Jonson makes the scene of his first humour comedy Italy. But for all this romantic *premise* the *conclusion* is invariably English. English lords masquerade as dukes of Pavia and Bologna. London fops and gallants, bawds and cheats, cut-purses and whores, religious fanatics, national heroes, and officers of state assume the incognito of French and Italian and Spanish names. But the acts and the emotions if not the situations and the names are pure English. There is preserved to us a complete panorama of English life from the stews on the Bankside to the Banqueting House at Whitehall. For completeness there is no body of literature like it. The mere fact that the form is dramatic means that the aspirations and the ideals, or the lack of them, the prejudices and the sympathies of all classes, literate and illiterate, are reflected in it.

The history of the evolutionary process which produced this realistic literature is one of the most fascinating stories in the domain of letters. The contributing factors were many and a complete study of them would take one far into causes which conjoined at this time to make England a new world-power. Most important among these factors to my mind, since I have chosen to study it, is the loss of didactic purpose which was, as I have observed, the predominant characteristic of early Elizabethan drama. Before plays could be written which would show men as they are, writers had to believe that this was a better thing to do than to show them as the church or any other regent of morals thought they should be.

Didacticism assumed two forms in Elizabethan drama. It provided first of all some means for guiding the understanding of the audience to a correct interpretation of the events pictured before it. In the miracles an expositor frequently rode beside the pageant to explain the significance of the Biblical stories enacted by the players. In early Tudor drama the expositor yields to the Prologue and Epilogue whose business it was to expel all doubts of the worthiness of the actors' enterprize. When neo-classical fashions in play-making were introduced the Chorus was often entrusted with the didactic utterances of the author.   In addition the various characters from time to time stepped out of their parts to sermonize or reassure the spectators that all would be well before the play was done.   It is this form of didacticism, its origin, development, and final disappearance from the drama which I have discussed at length in the first part of this essay.

But the moral purpose of the drama was maintained by another means, less direct and palpable.   The issue of the plot of most of the early plays was calculated to teach by example.   The original nature of many a foreign story was altered to make the end conform to the dictates of a rigid moral code.   To show the drama's gradual emancipation from this kind of didacticism I have examined with some detail two specific moral problems which have vexed humanity since the days of Eden: the relations between the sexes and the question of justice.   It is possible to observe in the case of the first a development which results finally in the splendid realism of *Othello* and the *White Devil* and the *Maid's Tragedy*.   With the second the transition is more abrupt, for Shakespeare's contemporaries at once abandoned the conception of justice which obtains in the early Tudor drama.   Yet there is some advantage to be gained in trying to find out precisely how this change was effected.

The study, then, of the decline of didacticism in theme and plot and the consequent triumph of realism constitutes the second part of my thesis.   I wish it had been possible, as I hope it will some day be possible, to carry this particular phase of the subject through the later years of Jacobean and Carolingian drama, for the exigencies of thesis-writing have necessitated setting a limit—1612.   Having once gained emancipation from the bonds of didacticism, the dramatists were not long content with presenting life as they saw it.   They began almost immediately to look for the unusual, the striking, even the grotesque and the equivocal.   The great fault of post-Elizabethan drama is not so much its immorality, for morality after all is a question of a particular moment in history, but its sensationalism, its narrow range of emotion, and its lack of contact with the whole of English life.

It is a pleasure to acknowledge here my especial gratitude to Professor T. M. Parrott for his supervision of this thesis.   His students know how lavishly his store of Elizabethan scholarship is set before them.   My thanks are also due Professor R. R. Cawley for his careful reading and correction of the manuscript.

CONTENTS

I

ASPECTS OF THE MORALITY TRADITION IN ENGLAND

The Churchmen of the Middle Ages from the beginning of the Christianization of Europe found themselves constantly embarrassed by the tradition of profane letters to which they, as the successors to the glory of Rome, were the natural heirs. Those sterner souls like Tertullian and Isidore refused the inheritance. Poetry for them is an invention of the devil. Isidore's pronouncement on the pagan poets does not vacillate: "The Christian is forbidden to read their lies."[1] Tertullian's *De Spectaculis*, in spite of the suspicion of heresy attached to its author, was rifled again and again by later writers for arguments against the deceitful fictions of the heathen. Men like Augustine who had been touched by the beauty of classical literature and who were accordingly reluctant to interdict it completely, advocated an allegorical interpretation by which the myths were to be considered symbolical of man's moral struggles and read solely for their preceptual value.[2] How well the medieval world learned to transmute moral allegory into poetry we may see in the *Divine Comedy*.

The problem of profane letters troubled many thoughtful men outside the orders of the church. The writers themselves, especially when the first days of the Rénaissance brought the necessity of a new compromise with pagan philosophy and poetry, often had serious doubts of the validity of their work. In this connexion there are no more interesting documents than Chaucer's famous retraction and Boccaccio's letter to Maghinardo de' Cavalcanti, written a little less than thirty years before. Chaucer at the end of the Canterbury Tales begs his readers to pray Christ to have mercy on him and forgive him his guilts, "and namely, of my translacions and endytinges of worldly vanitees, the whiche I revoke in my retraccions. . . ." All that he would leave for the world to enjoy are his Boethius and "othere bokes of Legendes of seintes, and

[1] Isidore's position is discussed by Ernest Brehaut in his study entitled *An Encyclopedist of the Dark Ages*, New York, 1912. pp. 74-75.

[2] J. E. Spingarn, *Literary Criticism in the Renaissance*, New York, 1899. Chapter I.

omelies, and moralitee, and devocioun" and such of the Tales as "sou-nen [not] into sinne." Boccaccio, writing to Cavalcanti some years after the admonitory vision of a Carthusian had nearly—it is one of the glories of Petrarch that it was prevented—persuaded him to abandon his books and take orders, repudiated his human comedy, the *Decamer-one,* and begged his friend not to increase his shame by allowing the women of his household to read the stories which, he says, can impel even "iron-hearted men to sin."

Even in the heyday of the Renaissance the ghosts of Tertullian and Isidore walked in the studies of the poets, crying out against their sin in revering or imitating the ancients. Sir Philip Sidney, one-time de-fender of the poet's art, "when his body declined," so Fulke Greville piously records, "and his piercing inward powers were lifted up to a purer Horizon . . . then discovered, not only the imperfection, but vanitie of these shadowes [his poems and the Arcadia] how daintily so ever limned, as seeing that even beauty itself, in all earthly complex-ions, was more apt to allure men to evill, than to fashion any goodness, in them."[3] The case of Milton is well known, how in his later years he turned away from the classical poetry which had been the delight and stimulus of his youth, charging the unscrupulous Greeks with plagiarizing from the Hebrew songs:

> Ill imitated while they loudest sing
> The vices of their deities, and their own,
> In fable, hymn, or song, so, personating
> Their gods ridiculous, and themselves past shame.[4]

But this is only half the story. Literature, like philosophy, early rescued from the service of the pagan deities, was given a new position as the handmaid of theology. The liturgical drama, obviously the most striking instance of the services rendered the church by the art of let-ters, is only one of the many types of medieval literature engendered by the theological impulse. Appearing first in rudimentary form in the tropes of the ninth and tenth centuries, the church drama grew in con-tent until upon its emergence from ecclesiastical control in the thirteenth it possessed a cosmic theme developed on a scale truly medieval in its grandeur. The church, though now officially rid of its troublesome servant, continued unofficially to assist the laymen in the yearly pres-entation. The London Guild of St. Nicholas, an organization of clerks,

---

[3] For more in this same vein, particularly Greville's remarks about Sidney's resolution to burn his Arcadia, see the *Life,* pp. 15-17, Clarendon Press Edition.

[4] *Paradise Regained,* IV, 339-342.

gave plays in 1384, 1391, 1409, 1411. Many churches sponsored performances independent of the guild cycles. Monks wrote the promptbooks for the guilds and as late as 1575 the Archbishop of York was asked to revise and correct the plays given in the cathedral city of his diocese. So long as the Roman church remained supreme in England the drama which it had fostered and continued to support was regarded as an instrument of good by the majority of laymen and clergy.[5] No matter how ungodly the antics of the wife of Noah and the Bethlehem shepherds may appear to the modern understanding, there seems little reason to doubt that the audiences in the market place and streets of York and Chester felt they were seeing something good for their souls, happy, in the Horatian phrase, to be profited and delighted at the same moment.

It is possible that by the end of the twelfth century the miracle plays were in some instances performed outside the church; the year 1200 may therefore mark the beginning of the secularization of the church drama.[6] With the moralities, by many regarded as an outgrowth of the miracles, the problems of origin are really insoluble. Mr. Thompson, arguing from the great use which the church made of allegory as a means of inculcating doctrine, supposes that they are of clerical origin and were designed to teach moral lessons as the miracle plays "purposed to teach the facts of sacred history."[7] This may well represent the intention of the individuals, no doubt in most cases clerics, who wrote the plays but proof is entirely lacking that the church, officially, stood sponsor to the morality. It first emerges in the miracle cycle, outside the church, notably in two pageants of the Coventry series—the Salutation and Conception and the Slaughter of the Innocents. The Paternoster Play at York "setting forth the goodness of the Lord's prayer" and the pageant of Vicious in the Beverley Show seem to be similar early examples of the form. And yet in spite of the fact that the morality when it appears in English dramatic history is a popular and not an ecclesiastical product, one

[5] This in spite of the Wycliffite sermon against miracle plays and the disapprobation expressed in some of Grosseteste's pastoral letters as well as other scattered references. These documents do not weigh against the evidence for clerical tolerance gathered by Chambers in chapters XXI and XXII of the *Medieval Stage*.

[6] The Anglo-Norman *Adam* is dated by its editor, Luzarche, in the late 1200's or early 1300's. The action takes place at the west door of the church, the audience standing, apparently, in the yard.

[7] E. N. S. Thompson, "The English Moral Plays," *Conn. Acad. of Arts and Sciences, Transactions.* Volume XIV, pp. 291-414.

must not suppose that anything but pleasurable edification was its object. The form even during the first twenty years of the sixteenth century is still dominated by theological abstraction.

The morality found favor from the start. The small number of actors required in its performance and the simplicity of the setting demanded—except in such spectacular examples as the *Castle of Perseverance* and Lyndsay's *Three Estates*—were factors certain to increase its popularity at a time when the guilds were finding the expense of mounting the Corpus Christi plays increasingly burdensome. The moral play, too, proved to have possibilities of expansion and development. In the sixteenth century, showing itself an able propagandizing instrument of various new forces of the age, it was employed to teach all manner of doctrine in theology, science, education, politics, and sociology. In the palace of the king, in the hall of the lord, the guildhall of the town and the courtyard of the inn small troupes of actors taught Nobility how to save the State and Commonalty how life must be ordered to deserve salvation. Apart from the miracles already disappearing in the middle of the century, the moral interludes furnished the bulk of the drama known to Englishmen for the medieval farce and the sottie, great favorites in France, seem never to have been domiciled in England. The significance of this fact for the subsequent development of the drama cannot be overemphasized. That it is a fact needs further demonstration.

The following statistics compiled from Mr. Chambers' abstract of the Stationers' Register will show at a glance the kind of plays which the publishers between the years 1557 and 1590 could obtain from their owners and thought capable of attracting trade.[8]

Total number of plays entered	79
(Lost plays	5)
Translations of classical drama	21
Moralities	25
Plays with morality features	9
Other didactic plays	3

The sixteen miscellaneous plays remaining include such various items as *Ralf Roister Doister, Jack Juggler, Gammer Gurton's Needle,* the four Senecan tragedies presented at the Law Inns, three plays of Lyly, and Peele's *Arraignment of Paris*.

It is true that this compilation does not take into account such innovations on the public stage as Kyd's *Spanish Tragedy* and the plays

[8] *Elizabethan Stage,* Vol. IV, Appendix L.

of Marlowe and Greene which were on the boards by 1590 or of the numerous plays on classical themes (the names of seven survive in the Revels Accounts) which were presented, chiefly at court, during this period. Nor does it, on the other hand, tell us anything about performances of other moralities which were popular in the provinces and, we may surmise, in the metropolis as well. What it does show is the predominance of the morality form in English drama long after the classical impulse from abroad had transformed other native literary forms.

With an independence characteristically British, classical and Renaissance stories were equipped with a Vice and occasionally with representatives of the Virtues as well and the tale in each instance given a moral turn it did not possess in the original form. In the *"newe Enterlude of Vice, Conteyninge the Historye of Horestes"* (printed 1567) it is the Vice, self-named Courage, who prompts Orestes to the murder of his mother. When the slaughter is over, Duty and Truth crown the avenger and deliver short homilies appropriate to the occasion. Haphazard, the Vice in *Apius and Virginia* (printed 1575), furnishes the mainspring of the action for it is he who suggests to the wicked judge a means of winning Virginia. Again the forces of righteousness close the play and point the moral. Fame, Doctrine, and Memory bear in the tomb of Virginia. Justice speaks:

Justice   And Justice, sure, will aid all those that imitate her life,
Reward   And Reward will punish those that move such dames to strife.

The *"Commodye of pacient and meeke Grissill"* (c. 1565) is similarly equipped with morality machinery. The courtiers attending on Gaultier bear the names Reason, Sobrietie, Fidance, Politicke Persuasion. The last named is essentially the Vice for he functions as Haphazard in *Apius and Virginia* and Ambidexter in *Cambises*, suggesting to the protagonist the evil he is to do. Grissill, during her time of exile, receives the ministrations of the Virtues, Constancy, Diligence, and Patience. The author has been largely influenced by the moralities of the *Nice Wanton—Lusty Juventus—Disobedient Child* variety for he presents his heroine as a model child, thoughtful of her parents and careful of her own honor. Various characters in the play have words to say about the bringing up of children, including, of all persons, the cruel husband who advocates frequent applications of the rod "in tender yeares, while youth is greene and fresh." The *"Lamentable tragedy mixed full of pleasant mirth, conteyning the life of Cambises King of Percia"* (registered 1569), a play which in Shakespeare's day became a synonym for rant and fustian, although it is the work of a university man familiar with Senecan tragedy, depends for the motivation of many of the acts of cruelty committed by the King and Judge Sisamnes on the subversive plotting of one Ambidexter, the Vice. Other abstract characters appear. The juxtaposition of morality figures with the Senecan tyrant makes this mirthful tragedy one of the oddest and at the same time most significant of Tudor plays.

The influence of the morality does not cease with the new era inaugurated by Marlowe and Shakespeare. Apart from the survival of the Devil and Vice, now become in every instance comic figures, the tradition can be seen in such plays as *The Cobbler's Prophecy* (c. 1594), *A Merry Knack to Know a Knave* (c. 1592), and *Two Lamentable Tragedies* (1594-1601). In the play last named the framework is provided by the machinations of Homicide, Avarice, and Murder. Truth opposes their schemes and assures them after the play is done and they are busy concocting new woe for mankind that she will be eternally vigilant in exposing them. Allegorical plays continued long popular at the universities although the occasionally witty *Lingua,* performed, it is supposed, at Cambridge soon after the turn of the century, retains little that is characteristic of the morality aside from the abstractions (the five senses, Appetitus, Commonis Sensus, Memoria, etc.) which serve as dramatis personæ.

Queen Elizabeth, whose literary tastes were catholic to say the least, witnessed a performance in 1601 of a morality called *The Contention between Liberality and Prodigality*. The old theme of the conflict between the Vices and the Virtues which formed the plot of the earliest moralities is here so changed as scarcely to be recognized. Seven songs are introduced to enliven the action; there are realistic scenes staged in front of the tavern with Tom Tosse and Dicke Dicer in prominence. Fortune is brought on in her chariot drawn by four kings—an evident reminiscence of the famous spectacle in *Tamburlaine* (II, IV, 4)—and the play closes with a very merry mock trial before Judge Equity. Nevertheless, in spite of its comic opera tendencies, *Liberality and Prodigality* is really a morality play. Prodigality as the chief of the forces of evil is sentenced and may escape death only if his sovereign, the gracious Elizabeth, wills to pardon him. Virtue triumphs; wrongdoing suffers and a moral lesson is intended.

The dominance of the native drama, and this means, practically, the morality, in the first thirty years of Elizabeth's reign can be more easily comprehended by a comparison of dramatic conditions in England with those which obtained in France. Medieval French drama was exceedingly rich and varied. Forms only slightly represented across the channel flourished in Paris and the provinces—the miracle, the farce, and the sottie, for example. The French morality had developed by the mid-sixteenth century in a number of directions and promised to evolve into a genuine national drama.[9] The historical moralities and especially the little moral dramas of bourgeois life such as *La pauvre fille villageoise* possess a charm and power superior to most of the English plays written before 1585. But circumstances were destined to halt the course of this nascent drama. In 1542 the Confrères de la Passion, asking permission to present a dramatization of Old Testament history, were attacked by the public prosecutor on the ground that their plays taught false doctrine. The brothers won their cause but theirs was the last performance of a religious play allowed by the authorities in Paris. In 1548 when the Hôtel de Bourgogne was opened they were given the exclusive right of performing in the city but their plays, the concession stipulates, must not touch religious matters or show any scenes contrary "aux exigences de la morale." Four years later the career of French classical tragedy officially began with the production of Jodelle's *Cléopâtre* at the court of Henri II. At a ceremony held after the performance the author was hailed as a hero, and a goat, wreathed with flowers and ivy, was solemnly devouted to Bacchus and brought to him to symbolize the great event which had taken place—the introduction of tragedy into France. Poets and patrons complimented him and the occasion received generally so much prominence that the older critics have been inclined to exaggerate its importance, holding that this was the veritable death-blow of the older drama. As a matter of fact the new Senecan drama, though extremely popular with the aristocrats and the academics, received little encouragement at first from the popular theater. The farce and the romance, a type of which *Huon de Bourdeaux* and *La destruction de Troie* are examples, maintained their vogue there. But gradually interest in the revival of tragedy spread to the public playhouses so that by the end of the century the course of French drama had been determined. The form and to a large extent the themes of Italian

---

[9] The number of moralities extant in France is about the same as in England. The list given by Mr. E. N. S. Thompson in his *English Moral Plays* contains a few less than the *Repertoire du Théâtre Comique en France au Moyen-âge* but he does not include the miracle-moralities of the *Ludus Coventriae*. One play, *Enough is as Good as a Feast,* has been discovered since his article was written.

tragedy were accomodated to the French taste and the nature of the subsequent drama fixed. M. Lanson, the most recent investigator of this rather vexed problem puts the case as follows "Il serait également faux de dater de cette année 1552 la substitution du drame antique aux genres du moyen âge sur la scène française et de reculer cette substitution aux environs de 1600, à l'epoque où des comédiens viendront présenter des tragédies et des tragi-comédies au public payant de Paris dans le local occupé jusque-là par les Confrères de la Passion. La vérité est que la chose ne se fit pas en un jour, que Jodelle commenca et n'acheva pas que Hardy et ses comédiens achevèrent ce qu'était commencé depuis un demi-siècle. . . . .[10] At first glance this might seem to parallel the condition which prevailed in England but such is not the truth. In France it was really the exotic trans-Alpine drama which eventually triumphed. It was in no way modified by the native dramatic condition. In England the plays constructed on the exact Senecan model—far fewer in number than those which saw production in France—never reached the public theater at all and while they influenced the young dramatists who saw them, it was the indigenous English drama which triumphed in the end by absorbing what was useful of the Senecan style and machinery. In other words the native tradition was strong enough through the fact that it received support from court, college, and public to control the course of English drama. This was true, it appears, of Spanish drama as well. French critics have in consequence looked with longing at these two more fortunate countries. M. Mortensen writes: "La part de l'influence antique dans ces pays, consista à ennoblir le style, à perfectionner l'art dramatique, mais elle ne fut pas assez exclusive pour détruire les traditions du drame national. En France au contraire les tentatives isolées . . . . etaient restées sans résultat pratique appréciable."[11]

Although the French morality before its career was halted had produced a number of modifications of the simple conflict type, it does not show the slow and orderly development characteristic of the English form. Before the appearance of Skelton's *Magnificence* (c. 1516) there is no English moral play with a secular theme; the French writers had realized long before this the usefulness of the dramatic allegory for

---

[10] G. Lanson, "Études sur les origines de la Tragédie classique," *Revue de hist. littl. de la France* (1903), pp. 177ff.

[11] M. Mortensen, *Le Théâtre français au moyen âge*, p. 192.

instruction in morality and statecraft as well as theology.[12]   But during the last years of Henry's reign and the next quarter century the English morality kept pace with the intellectual expansion of the country and became a truly national drama by reflecting the interests of the entire state.   The new religious doctrines were defended and refuted on the stage; the new learning is found strangely dramatized in such plays as *The Four Elements* and *Wit and Science*.   In so far as they dared, for the Tudor sovereigns were quite as jealous of their power as their Stuart successors, the dramatists discussed questions of government.[13] The dispossessed tenant, the poor farmer, and the oppressed laborer saw themselves represented in *Enough is as Good as a Feast* (c. 1560) and *All for Money* (printed 1578).   In fact most of the concerns which are nearest a man's personal life—his religion, his means of livelihood, the upbringing of his children, his interest in the affairs of the nation—are given some sort of dramatic treatment in the moralities.   Finally in the first thirty years of Elizabeth's reign the morality frequently has for its theme, not a precept borrowed from the dogma of the church or the creed of the advocates of good government, but some homely maxim, ethical in nature but familiar to the people through the problems of their daily life rather than the instruction of the church.

It is the plays of this kind which really characterize the English morality.   The old conflict between the vices and virtues, represented in its simplest form in *Hickscorner* and in its developed condition, with man as the object of the attack, in a dozen plays beginning with the *Castle of Perseverance,* the plays of the Coming of Death, the pedagogic dramas like *Youth* and *Mundus et Infans,* even the moralities of religious controversy or of political and economic theme can be largely duplicated in France.[14]   But of the "thesis" morality, if one may so designate the type, the French possess few examples.   M. de Julleville has described these few exemplars in words which fit the English plays as well.   "Toutefois l'intention de ces pièces est plutôt morale que re-

[12] The French favored one type of allegorical drama not to be found in England, a kind of morality *d'occasion*.   Two examples occur before 1500—*La Paix de Peronne* and *Concile de Bâle*.   *La condemnation des Banquets,* a secular morality, appears as early as 1507.

[13] Examples of political moralities: *Magnificence, King John, Respublica, Albion Knight*.   The last-named is extant only as a fragment.

[14] The best discussion of the English morality before 1520 is contained in the preface to Mr. Ramsay's edition on *Magnificence* in the E.E.T.S. series.   He not only classifies the plays but also notes the progress made in plotting and characterization by Skelton's time.

ligieuse; et elles semblent se proposer de former des honnêtes gens au sens mondain, plutôt que de pieux Chrétiens."[15]   There are five English plays pronouncedly of this type.

The earliest, *Enough is as Good as a Feast,* stands nearest to the strictly religious morality for the Prophet and God's Plague are there introduced to frighten wretched Worldly Man into a reformation which, however, is not effected for the sinner dies in his guilt and the Devil comes romping in to thank "his boy" Covetousness, for serving him so well and to carry the unrepentant offender off to Hell on his back.[16] But in spite of this somewhat Calvinistic machinery the theme is rather ethical than religious. Man should be contented with enough for his needs and not seek to enrich himself at the expense of others, in this particular instance the Tenant (a Cotswold character), the Servant, and the Hireling, all dependent on Worldly Man and all inhumanly treated by him.

W. Wager, the author of *Enough is as Good as a Feast,* seems to have had a fondness for plays with catch-titles.   One of them, *'Tis Good Sleeping in a Whole Skin,* ended this life in the famous fire started by Warburton's cook.   Another, *·The Longer Thou Livest the More Fool Thou Art,* may well be included in the category of instruction-to-youth plays, as the title-page suggests: "A very merry and Pythie Comedie . . . a Myrrour very necessarie for youth and specially for such as are like to· come to dignitie and promotion."   But there are modifications of the type which must be noted.   In the earlier plays with similar theme the chief character is a neutral figure led into sin by the forces of evil and later brought to repentance and reformation by the forces of good. *The World and the Child* is probably the best example of this simple form.   But Moros, the central figure in *The Longer Thou Livest* scarcely conforms to the type.   He is an Elizabethan clown, a braggart, and a poltroon.   Especially significant are his words at the close of the play. Although Judgment has struck him down and handed him over to Confusion who is to take him out and arrange for his transportation to Hell, he remains jauntily indifferent to the curses that rain upon him. To the horrible-visaged Confusion he says:

> Go with thee ill favored knave,
> I had lever thou wert hanged by the necke,
> If it please the Devil me to have,
> Let him carry me away on his backe.

[15] de Julleville, *La Comédie au moyen âge,* p. 48.

[16] The only copy of this morality in existence is at present in the Huntington Library, having been purchased at the Mostyn sale in 1917 when it emerged from oblivion.   It has been reprinted in facsimile by the library.

Even in plays like the *Nice Wanton* and the *Disobedient Child* which have largely lost their allegorical and theological elements there is no such bold speaking by the prodigals. In the former Dalila and her criminal brother Ismael repent before they die for their wickedness. The wanton son, the hero of the *Disobedient Child,* is compelled by the author to expiate his sins in his marriage to a shrewish wife but in spite of this judgment upon him he is ashamed of his former life and seeks and obtains his father's pardon. Wager provides no such conclusion for his morality. It is true God's Judgment delivers a short sermon with the preceding events as a text but this theme, developed naturally with certain theological variations as good sermons ought to be, is the folly of fools who refuse to learn what is good for them to know. Although the coloring of the play is pious, even Puritanical, the idea it dramatizes belongs rather in the realm of ethics than of religion.

The title of the next morality to be considered shows plainly its emancipation from strictly theological influence: *Like Will to Like quod the Devil to the Colier, very godly and full of pleasant mirth* (a formula applied indiscriminately to nearly every interlude) *Wherein is declared not only what punishment followeth those that wil rather followe licentious living, then to esteeme & followe good councel: and what great benefits and commodities they receive that apply them unto vertuous living and good exercise.* The author of the prologue plainly states the source of the text:

> The name of the matter, as I said whilere,
> Is Like will to Like, quoth the Devil to the Colier.
> Sith pithy proverbs in our English tongue doth abound,
> Our author thought good such a one for to choose,
> As may show good example, and mirth may eke be found. . . . .

The theme, therefore, in Pauline phraseology is "Evil communications corrupt good manners." The Vice, Nichol Newfangle, is enjoined by his godfather Lucifer always to couple like to like. A brave company of rogues, including Ralph Roister, Tom Tosspot, the cony-catchers Cuthbert and Pierce Pickpurse, gather about him, brought together by his deceitful promises of reward. Tom and Ralph in the end get a bag and a staff, that is to say, Beggars' Manor; the ruffians are presented with a halter and are dragged off by Hankin Hangman to the "land of the two-legged mare"—in polite language, the gallows. The Virtues are a negligible lot; their chief business consists in exchanging compliments and raising an occasional hymn to the Deity. The play was obviously enjoyed for its realistic scenes although the author, conforming to the tradition which required that the drama teach some kind of lesson, is particular in Tom's speech of repentance to admonish all parents to have respect to their children's associates lest their meed be eternal damnation for neglecting so important a duty.

The plot of George Wapull's *The Tyde Taryeth no Man* is contrived to show the fallacy of the old argument of the wastrel—*Bibamus dum vivimus.* The Vices employ this sophistical adage to encourage Hurtful-Help and Fayned-Furtherance to cheat their neighbors. By means of it Corage, the villain, convinces Willful Wanton, a maid who has but "seen the change of fourteen years," that marriage contrary to her mother's wishes is right and feasible for her. The forces of evil proceed unchecked in their villainy until Faithful Few, Authority, and Correction busy themselves in reform and begin to employ the Tide Tarrieth adage to "persuade people to turn from the error of their ways while there is yet time."[17] Again a dramatic fable making use of the entire allegorical machinery and even theological to a degree—Christianity is introduced in *propria persona*—presents a problem which vexes man frequently in his daily life: how is the sophistry of wicked men to be distinguished from true wisdom?

The last of these five "thesis" moralities, T. Lupton's *All for Money,* is less weighted with Calvinistic dogma than any of the others with the exception of *Like Will to Like.* The caption given by the publisher of the quarto of 1578 speaks in a new vein: *"A Moral and Pitiful Comedie, Intituled All for Money. Plainly representing the manner of men and fashion of the world noweadayes."* The vices are Money and his descendants, all born spectacularly before the eyes of the audience, Pleasure, Sin and Damnation. All-for-Money is set up as a magistrate and aids successively Gregorie Graceless, a ruffian and a thief, William-with-two-Wives, Nichol-never-out-of-the-law, Sir Lawrence, a foolish priest, and old mother Croote—all of whom receive his help only after they have presented a sufficient bribe. Gregorie wants to evade the consequences of the law, William to be rid of his wife, Nichol a piece of land owned by a poor man, Sir Lawrence a fat living, Mother Croote a young husband. Various characters—the total number is 32—bewail the corruption which money has wrought in them, reiterating the proverb, *monetas radix malorum.* Finally Damnation puts an end to the reign of Money, and the Virtues, Godly Admonition, Vertue, Humilitie, and Charitie conclude with the usual encomia of their own qualities. "Lupton seems to have entered on his work with the determination to drag in every type, individual, and abstraction that might serve to

---

[17] Mackenzie, *The English Moralities,* 1914, p. 187.

add an extra fragment of testimony on the evils of money."[18]   Only a
few of these have much importance in the plot but these half dozen
or so are among the most highly individualized of morality figures.
It is a pretty company of rogues that come to Money for aid—Nichol-
never-out-of-the-law, "like a riche frankeline, with a long bagge of
bookes by his side," talking of pleading and "tytles" and the very
ribald Sir Lawrence whose ignorance and general viciousness are such
common talk that even the little boys call naughty names after him in
the street.   The last of the suitors, the amorous Mother Croote, has
all the propensities but none of the wit of the Wife of Bath; William-
with-two-Wives is now and again taken up by the sheriff in these days.
It is comforting to know in this money-mad age that T. Lupton in 1578
saw England's greatness corrupted by the evil of greed.   Although one
may doubt whether this play represents, as he or his publisher claims,
the "manners of men and fashion of the world" of his day, it must be
admitted that he has illustrated an old saw with lively modern instances.

The Elizabethan moralities show an advance toward the realistic
drama of the later decades not only in the themes, which, as the foregoing paragraphs demonstrate, differ from those employed in the first
half century in being less often theological dogmas, but also in the increase in the number of typical and individualized characters.   In the
older moralities the associates of the Vice, the Taverner, the Dicer, and
lecherous Bessie, were almost the sole life-like characters to be found.
After 1558 this company of evil-doers is considerably augmented.   Cuthbert Cutpurse and Pierce Pickpurse, rogues from Fulwel's *Like Will to
Like,* boast of their achievements like rascals stepped from the pages
of one of Greene's pamphlets.   Tom Tosspot, from the same play,
swaggers in with a feather in his hat, swearing round oaths.   Let him
describe himself:·

> From morning till night I sit tossing the black bowl,
> Then come I home, and pray for my father's soul,
> Saying my prayers with wounds, blood, guts, and heart
> Swearing and staring, thus play I my part. . . . .[19]

Mercatore, an Italian merchant in the *Three Ladies of London,* is
a new arrival in English drama.   His creator, Wilson, puts in his mouth
the jargon of his trade, gives him a brogue much like that indicated for
Frenchmen in cheap comedies of the nineteenth century, and makes him

[18] Mackenzie, *op. cit.,* p. 199.
[19] Hazlitt's Dodsley, Vol. III, p. 6.

altogether such a bad fellow that he is willing to forswear the Christian religion that he may cozen a Jew.

Ignorant priests abound in these later plays. Since the authors, it would seem, are frequently ministers of the extremely Protestant persuasion, the characterization seldom shows the good-natured satire noticeable in early interludes like *The Pardoner and the Friar*. Sir Lawrence in *All for Money* has already been mentioned. He knows no Latin, Greek, or Hebrew; the new learning, he says, has destroyed all reverence that the common people once had for men of his class. When Sinne asks him how many chapters St. Matthew wrote in his Gospel, he shies at the question saying, "In other things [than reading the Bible] I have been occupied." Pressed to tell how many epistles St. Paul wrote after he was converted, he tries to bluster through with:

> By the masse he writ to manie, I would they were all burned,
> For had not they bene and the newe Testament in English
> I had not lacked living at this time I wisse . . . . (1286-1288)

Peter Pleaseman, the money loving clerk in *The Three Ladies of London*, has applied to Simony for the post of chaplain to Lady Lucre. When quizzed about his life and education, he admits he went to no university although at his college (a Roman seminary of course) he studies diligently for Lady Lucre's sake. "Of what religion are you," Simony asks. "Mary, sir, of all religions."

> Indeed I have been a Catholic; marry now for the most part a Protestant.
> But, and if my service may please her—hark in your ear, sir—
> I warrant you my religion shall not offend her.[20]

Elizabethan audiences dearly loved to see a foreigner made ridiculous on the stage. Satire of aliens had begun in the drama long before the days of the humour comedy. The early morality *Wealth and Health* introduces Hance, a drunken, boastful Fleming, to amuse the crowd with his tipsy tunes and garrulity.[21] But that is not the sole reason for his existence. The author vents on him the spleen of his countrymen who deplored the loss of English gold through the mercantile activity of the Dutch and the useless extravagance of the Dutch wars. Remedy says to him:

> Fie on the flattering knave
> fie on you aliaunts al I say

[20] Hazlitt's Dodsley, Vol. VI, p. 309.

[21] Entered in the Register the first year of its existence, i.e., 1557. This and the fact that it is printed in black letter makes it possible that it is an earlier play.

> Ye can with craft & subtel tiget [22]
> englishmens welth away.

Hance and Philip Fleming in *Like Will to Like* are much more entertaining fellows than this bellicose drunkard. Their master Tom Tosspot introduces them:

> . . . . and as for Flemish servants I have such a train,
> That will quass and carouse, and therein spend their gain. [23]

"Little-bellied Hance" enters presently so drunk he can scarcely stand. Newfångle, the Vice, persuades him to dance. But the fumes soon overcome him and after a few steps he tumbles, gets up groaning and is straightway asleep in his chair and snoring. Philip, on the contrary, is hardly characterized at all, the author not even troubling himself to indicate his Flemish accent.

There are other typical or exceptional characters in these later moralities which it would be interesting to discuss. Gerontus, for example, the kind-hearted Jew of the *Three Ladies of London* and the old Tenant speaking Cotswold in *Enough is as Good as a Feast*.[24] But a sufficient number have been mentioned to show how varied the persons of these plays are and how far toward realistic drama the morality had travelled by the third decade of Elizabeth's reign. There is one more significant element of this drama which must be considered, if one is to obtain any adequate notion of the reasons why the old native dramatic forms were still the favorites of the people, namely, the expression of patriotic sentiment found in it, a characteristic of Tudor drama usually supposed to have appeared first in the History Play. The midcentury *King John* is, of course, flagrantly chauvinistic although the sentiment is scarcely "pure" patriotism because the object of the dramatist is not so much the glorification of England as the villification of the Papal tyranny. Indeed patriotic utterance in the morality frequently takes the form of a "detractio." In Lyndsay's *Ane Satyre of the thrie Estaitis* one stage direction reads: "Heir enteris Flatteri, new landit out of France . . . ." In *The Three Lords and Three Ladies of London*, a late sequel to *The Three Ladies of London*, a play full of echoes of the Spanish war of '88, Simony in urging his vicious companions to join England's enemies,

---

[22] The text is very corrupt. This must be: Ye can with craft & subtelti get. . . . .

[23] Hazlitt's Dodsley, Vol. III, p. 325.

[24] The dialect characters and foreign types in Elizabethan drama have been thoroughly investigated by Herr Eduard Eckhardt and the results published in volumes 27 and 32 of Bang's *Materialen*.

says, "Tis not our native country, thou knowest, I, Simony, am a
Roman: Dissimultation, a mongrel—half an Italian, half a Dutchman:
Fraud so, too—half French and half Scotish: and thy parents (to
Usury) were both Jews, though thou wert born in London." But
Remedy in *Wealth and Health* speaks like some warrior king from a
History Play of the '90's:

> Consider Englishmen, how valiant they be and ferce
> Of al nacions none such, when they have their helth
> No land can do us harme, but wyth falsehood or stelth
> Remembre what nombre of men, or artilerie and good ordinance
> Specially ye grace of god, which is our chief forderance. (580-584)

Evidently the moral dramatists were quite as willing to satisfy popular
demand in this particular as we have seen them in the matter of realistic
scenes and individualized characters.

No matter how dull the modern reader may find these Elizabethan
moral plays, he must admit if he studies them at all carefully that they
present quite as faithful a picture of the interests and conflicts of that
age as the modern problem play does of our own. Not only had the
morality invaded the realms of science, theology, politics, and sociology
but it was busy with ethical questions approached from a secular rather
than a religious angle when the new dramatic epoch began in 1585.
Even the extremely controversial theological plays like *The Conflict of
Conscience* and *New Custom* mirror the alert enthusiasm of Elizabeth's
subjects for religious matters. What close study of this body of moral
plays reveals is not any poetry of excellence or any drama of more
than passable value; they are not to be studied as literature at all but
rather as documents of great sociological importance because they show
popular ideas and prejudices as no other documents surviving between
1550 and 1590. In a sense, and this may sound like extravagant heresy,
the late Elizabethan moralities express the whole tone of the times as
the later drama does not because, by 1590, the Puritans had left the
ungodly playhouses and exposed their views of life and morals henceforth only in pamphlets and sermons. Their case is no longer represented in the court of the theater.

It follows, naturally, since the morality is the typical dramatic form
of the Tudor reigns that the theory of the function of the drama held by
the writers of moral dramas was certain to prevail so long as their plays
were predominant on the stage. To say that the ministers of the gospel
and the pious laymen who wrote these plays always had a moral end in
view, is to be necessarily obvious. Literature was with them still, if not al-

ways the handmaid of theology, at least the servant of righteousness.[25] Even those plays which are most realistic merit salvation at the hands of the audience through their author's insistence that vice can be avoided only if it is cognizable and that their plays possess pedagogic value. But there existed a school of Puritan criticism which from the beginning sought to banish the drama, no matter how virtuous its lessons.[26] To such the writers were bound to offer some kind of apology of a more concrete nature. L. Wager in his prologue to *The Life and Repentance of Mary Magdalene* thus answers his detractors:

> (Let) no man in this point be offended
> In that vertues and vice we shall here introduce,
> For in men and women they have depended:
> And therefore figuratively to speake, it is the use.[27]

Does not his play "learnedly extoll vertue?" Doth it not teach God to be praised above all things? "What facultie doth vice more earnestly subdue?"

The author of *The Trial of Treasure* trusts:

> . . . . In our matter nothing you shall see,
> That to the *godly* may give any offense . . . .

Fulwel in the prologue to *Like Will to Like* explains that it is his purpose to please all men; yet no lascivious toys are to be found in his play. He bids his auditors:

> . . . . sith mirth for sadness is a sauce most sweet,
> Take mirth then with measure, that best sauceth it.

[25]Mr. H. L. Symmes (*Les débuts de la critique dramatique en Angleterre jusqu'à la mort de Shakespeare*) after a comparison of the morality prologues, summarizes his conclusions thus: "Le dessein ou but que l'auteur avait dans l'esprit en écrivant la pièce, est presque toujours exprimé et presque sans exception, toujours didactique. . . . . Quelquefois c'est un essai élaboré pour enseigner même la philosophie et la science. Plus souvent la morale de la pièce est expliquée avec précision. L'intention déclarée est tantôt d'enseigner directement tantôt par l'interprétation de l'exemple sur la scène. Assez souvent le but délibérément avoué est d'exciter l'auditoire à la réligion et, il y a même une pièce qui finit par un abrégé des commandments de Dieux [Bale's *Three Laws*]. Le plaisir et la joie simple sont le but de certains auteurs; mais plus souvent leur dessein est une conception générale de l'idée d'Horace; enseigner et amuser en même temps." pp. 47-48.

[26] See below in Chapter IV.

[27] Many of the prologues to the moralities, like those added to later plays, are the work of some writer not the author—apparently often an actor. But Wager is obviously speaking in person here.

The prologue to *Enough is as Good as a Feast* prays the pleasant muses to direct the actor's tongues to speak eloquently:

> Vertues to praise and to touch abuses,
> Dividing either of them plain and directly
> That it may appeer to all our audience evidently.

One more case will suffice to show how wary the dramatists were of offending the puritanic element in the audience by betraying the slightest inclination to condone vice. The long-winded prologue to *The Longer Thou Livest* concludes his account of the examples to parents furnished by his play with a word to the captious looking for things to censure:

> Holson lessons now and then we shall enterlace,
> Good for the ignorant, not hurtful to the wise,
> Honest mirth shall come in, and appear in place,
> Not to the advancement, but to the shame of vice,
> To extoll Vertue without faile is our devise. . . . .

The all-pervasiveness of the moral theory of the function of the drama during these years may be gaged conveniently by a glance at two of the later Elizabethan plays built around Italian themes but influenced in form by the morality. The actor who speaks for the company presenting *Apius and Virginia* exhorts all the members of the audience to hark well the tragedy. Let the wives imitate the blameless life they behold; let the pure virgins consider the glorious death for chastity's sake of the heroine.

> As she did wail, wail you her want, you maids of courtesy,
> If any by example here would shun that great annoy,
> Our Author would rejoice in heart, and we would leap for joy.

The Epilogue again urges the auditors to "take example"

> Of love to wife, of love to spouse, of love to husband dear,
> Or bringing up of tender youth. . . . .

The excessively humble "Preface" to John Phillip's *Pacient and Meeke Grissill* after apoligizing for the author's lack of "hawtie skill" begs his hearers to learn with Grissill "the Lord our God to praise." The "Postemus Actor," first making further apologies for the crudeness of the play (with good reason) and the acting, prays for the Queen and then for her Council that they may be so guided:

> That synne may be extirped and rooted out quight,
> And we unto truth and virtue, fyr our delight.

Finally the native tradition which required the drama to serve morality is to be seen in certain plays quite independent of the morality in form and at the same time uninfluenced by the classical revival in Renaissance drama and dramatic criticism. Although the *Historie of the two valiant knights Syr Clyomon Knight of the Golden Shield . . . . and Clamydes the white knight . . . .* contains nothing which could well edify an audience, being a garbled romance of the type travestied by Beaumont in *The Knight of the Burning Pestle,* yet the Prologue in advertising its contents feels called upon to justify his play in the conventional manner:

> Our Author he hath found the Glasse of Glory shining bright . . . .
> Wherein as well as famous facts, ignomius placed are:
> Wherein the just reward of both, is manifestly showne,
> That vertue from the roote of vice, might openly be knowne.

A Looking Glass for London and England by Lodge and Greene presents a lurid picture of the sins of Nineveh, elaborated on the basis of the Biblical Book of Jonah. Although the scenes of riot and sin, disclosed in all classes of society and pointed to by the prophets Oseas and Jonah as horrible examples for England, were no doubt relished for their own sake quite as much as for their value as bitter correctives, nevertheless the usurer restores the stolen goods, the King marries his mistress and all the sinners repent in time for the play to close in an odor of sanctity. Jonah concludes with a warning to Englishmen of the calamities awaiting them, calamities thus far averted only by the virtue of the Queen.

A Larum for London is of the same sort as *The Looking Glass.* Here a wretchedly dramatized pamphlet of Gascoigne's on the siege of Antwerp is presented to the citizens of London as a warning of the doom awaiting cities unregardful of the state of public morals. The Prologue, Father Time, promises them the play will,

> And if your hearts be not of adamant,
> Reform the mischief of degenerate minds
> And make you weep in pure relenting kind.

The old fellow appears again when the play is done, to repeat his admonitions and express the pious wish that it

> May be a meane all Cittyes to affright,
> How they in sinne and pleasure take delight.

Since the enormities of the Antwerpians seem actually to have consisted of nothing beyond a commendable desire to remain neutral in the Spanish war with the States-General, we may suppose that popular interest in the play was centered in the prevented rapes, the murders in cold blood,

the cruel deeds of Alva, and the nobility of the English governor. Nevertheless the audience is not allowed to leave without the satisfaction of
knowing it has been profited.

There is no need to labor the point further. If this lengthy review
of the morality of Elizabeth's time has fulfilled the law of its being,
it must make clear two facts: until 1585 the moral interlude dominated
English drama not because it was practically the only drama to be seen
but rather because by its adaptability to the changes in English manners and thought it was a truly national art-form, if so pompous a word
may be used of it. It follows from this fact that the Elizabethans were
bound to consider the drama's function that of moral instruction with
the delight of the audience a necessary but a secondary consideration.
What support or modification this theory received from the new literary
importations from Italy will be considered in the following chapter.

II

CONTRIBUTIONS OF THE RENAISSANCE

It is a fact so obvious as scarcely to bear repeating that the culture of the Middle Ages was classical, albeit many of the authors we now most venerate, particularly among the Greeks, were known only by name or from garbled passages quoted in the school grammars. It is quite as apparent, though less often considered, that the new classical learning which captivated Europe in the sixteenth century was interpreted by men whose philosophy of life and letters was medieval. There is no better instance of this fact than the body of commentary on the *Poetics* of Aristotle produced in the Italian Renaissance. The Middle Ages had little notion of what classical tragedies actually were. Dante's son, Pietro, thought a cantor recited them from a pulpit raised above the stage while below him the actors presented the story in pantomime;[1] Lydgate devotes eighty-odd lines of his *Troy Book* (II, 842-926) to a description of such performances "in the principal paleys" of Priam's city. As concerns their form, Donatus had decided that tragedies "exitus funesti habentur," a definition to be met with whenever a medieval writer is discussing the subject. Chaucer's Monk is merely repeating Donatus in metrical form when he says a tragedy is

> . . . . a certyn storie . . . .
> Of him that stood in greet prosperitee
> And is y-fallen out of heigh degree
> Into miserie, and endeth wrecchedly.   (B. 3163-3167)

The conception of tragedy as a narration in verse beginning happily and ending calamitously prevailed until the end of the fifteenth century. Tragedies in imitation of Seneca were written in Italy before that time but their authors intended them to be read, not acted.[2] It is of the use of tragedy as a work of instruction for the closet that Ascham is thinking when he writes in the *Schoolmaster:*

In tragedies, the goodliest argument of all, and for the use either of a learned preacher, or a civil gentleman, more profitable than Homer, Pindar, Virgil, and

[1] Passage in his *Commentary on the Divine Comedy*. Pertinent lines are given by Cunliffe, *Early English Classical Tragedies*, p. xvi.

[2] As early as 1315 Albertus Mussato wrote a tragedy, *Ecerinis*, for which he was crowned with laurel by the University of Padua.

Horace; yea comparable in mine opinion with the doctrine of Aristotle, Plato, and Xenophon; the Grecians, Sophocles and Euripides far overmatch our Seneca in Latin, namely in οἰκονομίᾳ et Decoro, although Seneca's elocution and verse be very commendable for his time. And for the matter of Hercules, Thebes, Hippolytus, and Troy, his Imitation is to be gathered into the same book, and to be tried by the same touchstone as is spoken before.[3]

The Italian critics of the sixteenth century—no one of whom dared die without having written a commentary on the *Poetics*—did much to clear away the medieval notion of the nature and function of dramatic writing, but they could not escape the philosophical inheritance which was theirs. This fact is especially evident in their understanding of the function of tragedy. Of the real meaning of Aristotle's definition there can scarcely be any disputing Butcher's interpretation. Tragedy affects the will only indirectly; its primary concern is with the emotions. The nature of its impression can perhaps be indicated by Goethe's words about the effect of Winckelmann's style upon his readers: "Man lernt nichts, aber man wird etwas." Except in the most general sense tragedy does not teach at all; nor does it conduce to morality by any effect which it exercises on the intellect. From the beginning the Italian critics missed the point. Even Averroes, whose commentary could have at least corrected the notion of tragedy as a narrated poem, if it had been translated before the Renaissance was in full swing, appears in the Latin version of 1552 as the champion of a moral purpose for tragedy. Speaking of the method of imitation peculiar to tragedy, he says: "Hoc autem fit imitando viros probos sanctitate atque puritate: quoniam imitatio fit de dispositionibus, quae virtutes inducunt, non de habilibus, cum hos imitari nequeamus." (Caput Quartum) The didactic function is clearly expressed. It becomes a commonplace in the criticism of the mid-sixteenth century. Geraldi Cintio, whose theories are to be found in practice in his dramas, declared the aim of tragedy and comedy is to conduce to virtue, one by terror, the other by jest. Trissino believed the office of the tragic poet is to admire and imitate the good, of the comic poet to mock the bad. Scaliger, who represents the extreme ethical position, declares tragedy should punish evil men and reward the good—a notion championed under the misnomer of Poetic Justice by such dissimilar English critics as Thomas Rymer and Samuel Johnson.[4] Scaliger on the func-

[3] *Works,* London, 1864, Vol. IV, pp. 228-229.
[4] I am indebted for these general facts to Mr. Spingarn's *Literary Criticism in the Renaissance,* Chapter III.

tion of tragedy at least, may be regarded as a spokesman for his age. In Chapter VIII of his *Poetics* he puts the problem in this way: "The result of the inquiry [whether the poet teaches character or action] is then that the poet teaches mental disposition through action, so that we embrace the good and imitate it in our conduct and reject the evil and abstain from that." [5] Such dissenters from the orthodox view as Castelvetro who endeavoured to give currency to a purely æsthetic theory of the function of the drama were cried down both by the dramatic poets and the dramatic critics. Cintio whose fame was perpetuated not only by his *Discorso de romanzi delle comedie e delle tragedie* but as well by romances and dramas written in exemplification of his theories, is a believer in Poetic Justice. "Ed il far morire . . . . o patir gravi mali è introdotto per più contentezza e per maggior ammaestramento di quelli che ascoltano, veggendo puniti coloro che erano stati cagione degli avvenimenti turbolenti, onde le mezzane persone erano state travagliate nella favola. . . . .[6] He would have no scenes of vice enacted on the stage, no vicious words spoken. In comedy if lasciviousness is imperatively demanded of a character, let it be so covered "col velo delle parole oneste che anco delle pulcelle potrà essere senza biasimo udita." In concluding the discourse Cintio reasserts that tragedy "tragge gli animi alla attenzione e gli empie di maraviglia, la quale gli fa bramosi di apparare. . . .quello che non sanno, cioé di fuggire il vizio e di seguir la virtù." [7]

Giovan Giorgio Trissino, first maker of tragedies in endecasillabi sciolti (the parent of English blank verse), dares offer the edition of his *Sophonisba* to Pope Leo X since, as he says in the dedication, "la Tragedia muove compassione e tema, con le quali, e con altri ammaestramenti arreca diletto a gli ascoltatori, et *utilitate al vivere umano*."[8] Relying on Aristotle who, he says, places tragedy above the other forms of poetry because it is ordained "per imitare con suave sermone una virtuosa, e perfetta azione. . . ." Trissino sets forth in this dedication a didactic theory of the drama to which he no doubt believed he was giving concrete form in the *Sophonisba*. In his dedication of *I Simillimi* to Cardinal Farnese he reiterates the theory, this time in an attempt to distinguish between comedy and tragedy: "E perchè la Tragedia

[5] Excerpt from the translation by F. M. Padelford in *Yale Studies in English*, Vol. XXVI, p. 83.

[6] *Discorso*, Milano, 1864, p. 35.

[7] *Ibid.*, p. 120.

[8] *Tutte le opere di Giovan Giorgio Trissino*, Verona 1729, Vol. I, p. 300.

imitando lauda, et ammira gli atti virtuosi, e la Commedia imitando dilegia, e vitupera i viziosi, avvieni, che a questo modo a una e al 'altra, ci insegnano la virtu." [9]

Out of a false interpretation of Aristotle, a medieval moral theory of poetry which made literature the handmaid of theology, and doctrine developed from the Horatian precept "aut prodesse volunt aut delectare poetae," the critics and dramatists of the Italian Renaissance constructed their theory of the function of the drama. This they passed on in turn to France and to England.

But the critical literature of the Elizabethan period had established the moral standard as the principal criterion of judgment some years previous to the arrival in England of the Senecan drama with its concomitant critical dogmas. Nor was this prevalent moral standard erected entirely on the basis of a tradition—as in the case of the moralities—which had its foundation in theological sanction. Neo-Classical theories helped to support it. Udall's prologue to *Ralph Roister Doister*, for example, defends his play on Horatian principles;

> The wise Poets long time heretofore,
> Under merry Comedies secrets did declare,
> Wherein was contained very virtuous lore,
> With mysteries and forewarnings very rare.

The fifth book of *A Woorke of Joannnes Ferrarius Montanus touchynge the good orderynge of a commonwealth*[10]—a typical Renaissance treatise on statecraft—considers the drama one of the seven handicrafts in a commonwealth. Good plays presented by honest actors the author believes are allowable. But the spectators must view everything allegorically, extracting the good as a bee sucks honey from noxious herbs.[11] "Ainsí quand vous entendez comment Pamphyle est ravi par l'amour de Glicère, et comment le vieux Chrèmes est en colère parce que sa fille est dédaignée, vous devez penser à l'instant en vous même quel honteux approbe c'est que d'être lié par les liens de Vénus."[12] The absurd antics of a boaster should purge vainglory from your system. The ravings

---

[9] *Ibid.*, p. 328.

[10] Translated from the *De Republica bene instituenda Paraenesis* in 1559 by William Bavande. Since the Princeton Library has no copy, I have relied on excerpts given by Symmes, *Les débuts de la critique dramatique en Angeleterre*, Paris, 1903, pp. 57-59, and a brief extract in Chambers, *The Elizabethan Stage*, IV, p. 190.

[11] This figure is a favorite with humanistic defenders of the stage. It is derived ultimately from Plutarch.

[12] Symmes, p. 58.

of Hercules (is he thinking of Seneca's *Hercules Furens?*) should teach you how offensive it is to displease God and excite his indignation. Not content with the allegorical argument alone Ferrarius rests a part of his contention on the Horatian theory. His criticism deserves particular attention because it appears in England just before the beginning of a new dramatic epoch and especially because it is the fullest treatment of the problem by any of the humanists of the Renaissance. Erasmus, Vives, Bucer, Elyot had found a place for the drama in their scheme of life—all of them admitting it, with careful reservations—among the fit instructors of youth.[13] With them, as with Ferrarius, the argument by way of justification is always the same: the value of the drama in the making of the wise and good man. Not once does any theory remotely æsthetic or even frankly hedonistic like Castelvetro's appear during these years.

The use of the moral argument in the justification of the art of letters is by no means confined to the drama during the Tudor age.[14] It was the custom of the translators and collectors of Italian novelle to introduce their amorous tales with some kind of moral apologia. Brooke, for instance, who betrays a too evident interest in the raptures of his Romeus and Juliet, addresses his readers in the following fashion: "To this ende (good Reader) is this tragicall matter written to describe unto thee a coople of unfortunate lovers, thralling themselves to unhonest desire, neglecting the authoritie and advise of parents and frendes, conferring their principall counsels with dronken gossyppes and superstitious friers (the naturally fitte instumentes of unchastitie) attemptyng all adventures of peryll, for thattaynyng of their wished lust,

---

[13] Erasmus would have Plautus expurgated. Vives would extend the process to Terence. Bucer urges the writing of comedies and tragedies on Biblical subjects and offers detailed suggestions for plots in his *De honestis Ludis* (1551).

[14] Although in a consideration of Elizabethan dramatic theory the body of criticism pertaining to poetry, which had reached considerable proportions by 1590, cannot be disregarded, it has seemed best in the interest of unity to omit here a discussion of Renaissance criticism in general. The defense of their enterprise by the translators of novelle is cited since the Italian tales furnished a source for later dramatic production. The question of the relative importance of didactic and aesthetic theories of the fine art in Elizabethan poetic criticism is adequately discussed by Mr. Guy Thompson in his Chicago dissertation, *Elizabethan Criticism of Poetry*, pp. 112-140. He demonstrates conclusively, what one might easily surmise, that the Elizabethans held the moral function paramount although some practitioners of the art, Sidney among them, placed the aesthetic first.

usyng auriculer confession (the key of whoredome and treason) and furtheraunce of theyr purpose, abusyng the honorable name of lawefull mariage, to cloke the shame of stolen contractes, finallye, by all meanes of unhonest lyfe, hastyng to most unhappye deathe."[15]   Brooke's parting words offer an inescapable argument.   All who read his poems and take the matter to heart "shall deliver my doings from offence and profit yourselves."

The locus classicus of such moral prolegomena is Fenton's dedication of his *Tragical Discourses* to the bluestocking patroness of letters, Lady Mary Sidney.   His essay possesses peculiar interest through its similarity in tone and argument to the much more famous treatise by Lady Mary's brother.   To both men history furnishes a treasury of precedents for the conduct of life.   But to both the work of the writer of fiction can be of greater service to the world than that of the historian for he can so order events that men will learn from his simulated histories to eschew evil.   "Histories [Fenton means, of course, tales like those in his volume] do swarme with examples of all kinds of vertues, wherein both the dignitye of vertue and fowleness of vice appereth muche more lyvelye then in any morall teachyng;   seyinge therein is figured under certeine formes and shaps of men and their doyngs past al and every such diversitye and change, which philosophie doth teach by waie of preceptes. . . . ."[16]   Like Bavande, the above-mentioned translator of Ferrarius, Fenton urges the extracting of a knowledge of good from the contemplation of evil.   How else may his readers consider the folly of foolish lovers, the "impudency of a maide or other woman renouncynge the vowe of her fayth or honor due to virginitie" or a dozen other vain doings pictured in his collection?   Fenton's arguments were not without effect in convincing some, at least, of his purpose.   Commendatory verses prefixed to his collection praise him as a servant of morality.

Apparently this method of gaining popular sanction for the publication of romantic stories was an Italian fashion.   Cintio in dedicating his *Gli Hecatommithi* to the Pope qualifies his work as condemnatory to vice and calculated to instruct in life and manners.   The proemio begins with the standard Renaissance statement of the instructive value

[15] *The Tragical Historye of Romeus and Juliet, written first in Italian by Bandell, and nowe in Englishe by Ar. Br.*, reprinted in *Shakespeare's Library*, ed. W. C. Hazlitt, London, 1875.   Part I, Vol. I, p. 72.

[16] *Certaine Tragicall Discourses* . . . . by Geffraie Fenton, reprinted in *The Tudor Translations*, Vol. XIX (First Series) pp. 4-5.

of literature. Life is varied; it is difficult to know which way to turn; counsel is needed by the unwary. Whence Cintio has concluded that this gift of writing was given to us chiefly that we may warn others of the pitfalls on the road of life, showing them how to escape from the labyrinths where often we lose the direct road and go wandering about like blind men. Man has been given freedom to elect what he will do but unless he receives some instruction, "avvertimenti fedeli e da una lunga isperienza," he is likely to go sadly wrong in his choosing. For these reasons the author has been led to write the stories which follow that they may serve as the faithful and well-grounded advice "which bewildered mankind needs."[17]

This digression has taken the discussion far afield but it has served, I hope, to show to what extent the humanistic theory of the function of literature—the theory which is best exemplified in the *Faerie Queene* —had permeated English literature by the time classical tragedy arrived in the '60's. The critical theories imported with Seneca really differ very little from these already in use by the defenders of the drama. But the new impulse reached England at the time when the first Puritan attacks were putting fear into the hearts of the playwrights. Because their words of defense were uttered under the stress of combat and are not the careful judgments of scholars or genial authors of books on the education of youth, the apologies of the translators or imitators of Seneca will repay rather careful scrutiny.

The Seneca whom Dante called "morale" and whose influence on Elizabethan drama is scarcely to be estimated by a tabulation of his *sententiae* found imbedded in different plays or in the evidences of Senecan form and dramatic convention in the native drama, was apparently looked upon by the puritanical as a vicious writer. His translators found immediate necessity of forfending attack. Verses prefixed to Studley's version of the *Agamemnon and Medea* (1566) speak of those backbiters who will discourage the author from "further fruits of wit." Let them know that Seneca is instructive reading; that his horrors are means of admonitions.

> Learne here to lyve a ryght and know
>   how that thear is a god,
> That well deservers well rewardes,
>   and ill, doth scurge with rod.

---

[17] The title-page of the 1565 edition reads: *Hecatomithi, overo cente novelle di M. Giovabattista Giraldi Cinthio, nobile Ferrarese; nelli quali altre dilletevoli materie, si conoscono moralità utilissime a gli huomini per il ben vivere & per destare altresi l'intelleto all sagacita. . . .*

For to thys and [end] is thys compylde
thys play thou hast in hand,
In vertues race to make thee run,
and vyce for to with stand.[18]

Studley, himself, in his dedication of the *Medea* to Lord Russell, calls his author "that pearless Poet and Most Christian Ethnicke Seneca, wherein no glutting, but swete delectacion, is offered unto ye mind that doth hunger after vertue."[19]

By 1581 the Puritan attack had begun in earnest with the publication in 1576 of Northbrooke's *Dicing, Dancing, Vaine Playes or Enterludes,* Gosson's *School of Abuse* in 1579, and Munday's (?) *Second and Third Blast of Retrait from Plaies and Theatres* in 1580. Preachers like White and Stockwood had denounced the ungodly theaters from the pulpit at Paul's Cross. Small wonder that Thomas Newton in bringing out *Seneca, His Tenne Tragedies, Translated into English* in 1581, should think it wise to defend his enterprise in a dedication to Sir Thomas Henneage, Knight, Treasurer of her Majesty's Chamber:

And whereas it is by some squeymish Areopagites surmyzed that the readinge of these Tragedies, being enterlarded with many Phrases and sentences literally tending (at the first sight) sometime to the prayse of Ambition, sometyme to the mayntenaunce of cruelty, now and then to the approbation of incontinencie, and here and there to the ratification of tyranny, can not be digested without great danger of infection: to omit all other reasons, if it might please them with no forestalled judgment to mark and consider the circumstances, why, where, and by what manner of persons such sentences are pronounced, they cannot in any equity otherwise choose, but find good cause ynough to leade them to a more favourable and milde resolution. For it may not at any hand be thought and deemed the direct meaning of SENECA himselfe, whose whole wrytinges . . . . are so farre from countenauncing Vice, that I doubt whether there be any amonge all the Catalogue of Heathen wryters, that with more gravity of Philosophicall sentences, more waightyness of sappy words, or greater authority of sound matter beateth down sinne, loose lyfe, dissolute dealinge and unbrydled sensuality. . . . .[20]

Gorboduc, the first of a line of Senecan plays in English, established for itself an enviable reputation as an instrument for virtuous instruction. The authors, Lord Buckhurst and Thomas Norton, show by their other works their belief in the moral function of literature. Buckhurst two years after the production of the play at the Inner Temple contri-

[18] Studley's Translations of Seneca's *Agamemnon and Medea,* edited by E. M. Spearing, Bang's *Materialen,* Vol. XXXVIII, p. 9.

[19] *Ibid.,* p. 124.

[20] *Seneca his Tenne Tragedies translated into English,* reprinted in Publications of the Spenser Society, Nos. 43 and 44, pp. 2-3.

buted to the *Mirour for Magistrates* one of its most famous "tragedies." The didactic purpose of the *Mirour* is evident from its title-page: "The Mirour for Magistrates wherein may bee seene, by examples passed in this Realme with how greevous plagues vices are punished in great Princes and Magistrates: and how fraile and unstable worldly prosperity is found where Fortune seemeth most highly to favour." (1587) Thomas Norton published, in the year of the play's production, Calvin's *Institutes*.[21] The following year the Psalter in English was issued, containing twenty-eight metrical renderings by him.

With two such authors *Gorboduc* could scarcely be other than a moral play. Their ulterior motive was a delicate suggestion to the Queen that she arrange a marriage for herself or at least fix the succession. But the moral of the play is evident. "The dominant idea of the whole seems to be that the laws of kind, i.e. human nature, must be obeyed, and that due control or restraint is necessary for all, whether for youths, subjects, or rulers; in the midst of the darkest days comes the repeated conviction that:

> Right will always live, and rise at length,
> But wrong will never take deepe root to last." [22]

Sir Philip Sidney, though he found the play "defectious in circumstances," in place and time, the "two necessary companions of all corporal action," did not withhold his praise for its value as a pleasurable sermon. "It is full of stately speeches and well-sounding phrases, climbing to the height of Seneca, his style, and as full of notable morality, which it doth most delightfully teach and so obtain the very end of poesy. . . . ."[23] Had it been perfect in the matter of the unities it might have remained "an excellent model of all tragedies."

---

[21] It may seem incongruous that a translator of Calvin should be a playwright. But Calvin, himself, was no fiery opponent of the stage. During his rule at Geneva he frequently permitted performances against the wishes of the Elders.

[22] *Gorboduc*, edited by L. T. Smith, Heilbronn, 1883, p. xix. This is obviously not Senecan but Christian morality. Seneca's philosophy agreed with the medieval doctrine that life in this world is evil and that escape from it is the highest good. But whereas the church taught that the doers of ill shall suffer hereafter unless they show penitence, Seneca was content with depicting, as horribly as possible, the vanity and misery of this world with the corollary that suicide is allowable if Fortune does not dispatch one before the burden of living becomes intolerable. By no means is the final triumph of Justice to be expected.

[23] *Defense of Poesy*, ed. by A. C. Cook, p. 47.

George Gascoigne, like the authors of *Gorboduc*, had dedicated his muse, at least after his rather spectacular conversion from the follies of his youth, to the cause of moral instruction. In 1575, after his return from Holland, he published an expurgated edition of his works, adding to it shortly an outrageously moral play, *The Glass of Government*, a moral satire, a translation of Innocent III's *De Contemptu Mundi*, and a pamphlet of obvious import, *A Delicate Diet for Daintie Mouthde Droonkardes.*[24] Ten years earlier he had experienced a similar access of conscience at which time "he determined to abandone all vaine delightes and returne unto Greyes Inn, there to undertake againe the studdie of the common Lawes." It was during this period of his first reformation that Gascoigne translated with Kinwelmersh the *Giocasta* of Lodovico Dolce and palmed it off on the superficially learned company of the Inn and the Court as pure Euripides. Since the translators follow their original line for line, expanding but never originating ideas or figures, it is impossible to determine from the text whether they regarded the play as a purge to the emotions or a sermon by example. But the glosses added by Gascoigne to the printed edition show how he intended the readers should view it. The precepts imbedded in the dialogue are noted, one after the other. Baillo's advice to Antigone (I, 3) is glossed as "a glasse for yong women." *Sententiae* like the following are drawn from the text—"Hope the help in miserye;" "Rehearsall of olde grudges doth hinder al reconciliation;" "Truth pleadeth simply when falsehood useth eloquence;" "If the head be evill the body cannot be good." The lament of Oedipus (V. 5, 199ff.) is foot-noted, "A glasse for brittel beautie and for lusty limmes." But the audience gathered in the hall at Gray's Inn were not left in doubt about the moral significance of the misery that had just been enacted before them. The epilogue to the play, written by Christopher Yelverton, makes all clear. Ambition brings men low; the golden mean, let them be sure, "the happie doth suffise."

---

[24] The three prefaces, *To the Reverende Divines, To al Yong Gentlemen, To the Readers Generally,* profess the author's purpose in this publication of his works. "I protest . . . . my desire hath bene to content most men: I mean the divine with godly Hymnes and Psalmes, the sober minde with morall discourses, and the wildest will with sufficient warning." *The Complete Works of George Gascoigne,* ed. by J. W. Cunliffe, Cambridge, 1907, ch. I, p. 16. It is significant that Gascoigne placed the *Jocasta* among the "Herbes to cure" and not among the "Floures to comfort" or "The Weedes to be avoided."

> Cease to aspire then, cease to soare so hie,
> And shunne the plague that pierceth noble breastes.
> To glittering courtes what fondness is to flie,
> When better state in baser towers rests?[25]

Gabriel Harvey who never praised anyone for anything he wrote unless there was moral matter in it, found words for Gascoigne's translation: "An excellent tragedie: full of many discreet wise and deep considerations."[26]

Gismond of Salern in Love, or *The Tragedie of Tancred and Gismund* as R. Wilmot named the play in issuing his augmented edition in 1591, is the first English tragedy from an Italian source—the first novel of the fourth day of the *Decamerone*—written in the Senecan manner. Boccaccio, one fears, would not recognize his own story so thoroughly was it made over in accordance with English standards of morality. Gismunda has become the sinning woman, beautiful and pitiful, but none the less a reprobate. Yet the authors evidently felt some trepidation in offering so lusty a play to the delicate ladies of the court. The sonnets—*Of the Queenes Maydes*—which preface the Landsdowne MS. make it quite plain that there is no imputation on their honor meant therein. Nor is there any glozing of Gismunda's moral delinquency:

> . . . . loe here for yow againe
> Gismondes unlucky love, her fault, her woe,
> And death at last, here fére and father slayen
> Through her missehap . . . .[27]

The Epilogus told the audience at Greenwich they need have no fear lest mad "Megera" pursue them. "Nor Pluto heareth English ghostes complaine our dames dizteined lyves." But he bids these same ladies to live:

> So as our Britain ghostes, when life is past,
> May praise in heven, not plaine in Plutoes hall
> Our dames, but hold them vertuous and chast . . . .[28]

When Wilmot in 1591 revised the play for the press he had been nine years the rector at North Okenham in Essex. Naturally he took pains to defend his unclerical proceeding. In his foreword to the Gentlemen of the Temple he recalls Beza's publication of his *Abraham* and

[25] Cunliffe's, *E.E.C.T.,* p. 159.
[26] A note written by Harvey in his own copy of the *Jocasta.*
[27] Cunliffe's *E.E.C.T.,* pp. 163-164 ll. 6-9.
[28] *Ibid.,* p. 216, ll. 26-28.

Buchanan's "most pathetical Jephtha" as precedents in his favor. Gismund shall stay close within the walls of the Temple, safe from the "tragedian tyrants of our time who are not ashamed to affirm that there can be no amorous poem savour of any sharpness of wit, unless it be seasoned with scurrilous words." He affirms the moral intent of the play, declaring it "tendeth only to the exaltation of virtue and suppression of vice, with pleasure to profit and help all men, but to offend or hurt no man." In the dedication to Lady Mary Peter and Lady Anne Gray, Wilmot says he is persuaded "there is nothing more welcome to your wisdoms than the knowledge of wise, grave, and worthy matters, tending to the good instructions of youths, of whom you are mothers." What, one wonders, would Bocas think of this—his pitiful tale of Gismunda presented to English matrons as a book of instructions for their young offspring!

The last of the four Senecan tragedies which the Law Inns contributed to early Elizabethan drama, Thomas Hughes' *Misfortunes of Arthur* (1599), has a patently Senecan moral, the vanity of this world's fortune and the deceitfulness of power and riches. From the magnificently Greek theme, which the author apparently hoped would stir the imagination of his English audience, of the curse upon the House of Arthur, Hughes is able to draw only this rather tame moral which the Epilogus in fifty lines drives home like a preacher:

> Short is the race, prefixed is the end,
> Swift is the tyme, wherein man's life doth run.
> But by his deeds t'extend renowne and fame,
> That onely vertue workes, which never fades.[29]

The audience with these words sounding in their ears could make no mistake in their lesson. But Nicholas Trotte of the Society, who wrote the introduction by which the play was presented to the Queen with the usually ingenious contrived flatteries, tells them again, in a kind of aside, precisely how to construe it:

> The matter which we purpose to present,
> Since streights of time our liberty controules
> In tragike note the plagues of vice recounts.[30]

The progress of Seneca on the Elizabethan stage has been frequently retold and his influence sighted in the works of Shakespeare, Marlowe,

[29] Cunliffe, E.E.C.T., p. 292, ll. 47-50. These last four lines are a curious mixture of Senecan and Christian philosophy, as, indeed, is the play itself.
[30] Cunliffe, *E.E.C.T.*, p. 223, ll. 127-129.

Greene, Marston, Chapman, Jonson, and even Beaumont and Fletcher.[31] Only one aspect of this tradition is of concern at this point. What became of the moral purpose which, as the discussion above has indicated, the earlier writers of Senecan drama considered the reason for their productions? The answer is simple: it disappeared. The "tragedy of blood" or the "revenge play," the logical successors of the early Seneca, is amoral, avowedly so; "there is no thought of picturing the avengers as more amiable or more noble minded than their victims. The tone of the play is frankly that of the vendetta and the author accepts savage conditions as he finds them without essaying any interpretation of life's problems."[32] The fault, one may add, is not wholly Seneca's. Marlowe who set London talking by his man-and-God-defying heroes was more endebted to Machiavelli, or better the makers of the myth about his, than he was to Seneca.

Of the external changes made in preparing Seneca for popular exhibition the most conspicuous is the abolition or restriction of the Chorus. At one stroke the best medium for the conveyance of moral precepts derived from the action is done away with.[33] In the early translations the process was already begun. Neville in his *Oedipus* consistently curtails the lines allotted the chorus and after the second act omits them entirely. Heywood's statement (preface to his *Troas*) is significant: "Alteracyon may be borne with all, seeing that the Corus is no part of the substance of the matter." Remnants of the moralizing chorus may be detected, however, in some of the earlier Senecan plays intended for the popular stage. In *Locrine*, for example, a few lines of moral comment are intrusted to Ate who acts as stage manager, getting the Dumb Show in and serving as Prologue and Epilogue. She speaks (IV, 2) after Albanact's ghost has appeared, in her capacity as expositor:

> Loe, here the gift of fell ambition,
> Of usurpation and of trecherie!
> Loe, here the harmes that wait upon all those

[31] C. F. Tucker Brooke, *Tudor Drama*, Boston, 1911, Chapter VI.

J. W. Cunliffe, *Influence of Seneca on Elizabethan Tragedy*, New York, 1907, pp. 54-126.

Cunliffe, *Early Classical Tragedies*, Oxford, 1912.

F. L. Lucas *Seneca and Elizabethan Tragedy*, Cambridge, 1922, Chapter V.

[32] Brooke, *Tudor Drama*, p. 210.

[33] The modifications of their originals made by the translators are discussed by Charlton and Kastner, *The Poetical Works of Sir William Alexander*, Vol. I, pp. clv-clviii.

> That do intrude themselves in others lands,
> Which are not under their dominion. (93-97)

Again in a few lines at the close of the play she warns the beholders to mark well the consequences of lust and ambition.

But as a general rule in the revenge play the audience is left to draw what conclusions it well may from the riot of passion and bloodshed mimicked on the stage. The most famous of the whole lot, *The Spanish Tragedy,* ends on a note of dire fatality. The Ghost of Andrea recounts with evident relish the murders consummated, Revenge promises to hale "downe to deepest hell" the foes who still remain, and departs with his grisly companion:

> To place thy freendes in ease, the rest in woes;
>   For herre, though death hath end their miserie
> Ile there begin their endless Tragedie.[34]

But the Stoic Seneca, whose philosophic writings were reverenced during the Middle Ages by the strictest of orthodox churchmen and who became in the fourth century the victim of a pious fraud which ascribed to him a series of letters to St. Paul, the "Seneca morale" of Dante, "of moralitee . . . . the flour," continued to exert a beneficent influence in the pseudo-dramatic writings of a group of English gentlemen of letters who scorned the public stage during the years of its greatest flourishing.[35] It was no less a person than Lady Mary Sidney who inaugurated the writing of Senecan closet dramas by a correct but frigid translation of Garnier's *Marc Antoine.* Samuel Daniel added as a pendant to her enterprise an original *Cleopatra.* Some years later (1605) he printed a drama possibly intended for the stage, *Philotas,* dedicating it to Prince Henry. Fulke Greville, friend of Sidney and Daniel and one of the Lady Mary's circle, added two long, pronouncedly Calvinistic plays to the roll. A third play on the Cleopatra theme he destroyed: "The executioner the author himselfe. Not that he conceived it to be a contemptible younger brother to the rest but lest while he seemed to looke over much upward, hee might stumble into the Astronomer's pit."[36]—which being interpreted means that Greville had no mind to be mixed up in any conspiracy charge through misinterpreted speeches in his play. In the north the Earl of Stirling, Sir

---

[34] IV, 5, 46-48. The morality of the popular Senecan drama will be discussed below in the chapter on Justice in Elizabethan drama.

[35] For some account of Seneca's fame in the Middle Ages see R. M. Gummere's *Seneca* in the series *Our Debt to Greece and Rome.*

[36] *Life of Sir Philip Sidney,* Clarendon Press edition, pp. 155-156.

William Alexander, worked over and revised, during a period of more than thirty years, his four *Monarchicke Tragedies,* having dedicated them originally to a famous student and practitioner of statecraft, James I of England. Last but not least, considered from the objective of moral content, is Samuel Brandon's *The Tragicomoedi of the vertuous Octavia,* a play with a mysterious origin and certainly never intended for production.

The nine original dramas in this list have one element in common, their didacticism. This point cannot be fully developed here, for the plays, interesting as literary curiosities and in the case of Daniel of considerable literary merit, are, after all, quite without influence in English dramatic history. Accordingly only a few examples illustrative of their moral trend can be given. Daniel's Cleopatra, though by no means the vampire of popular myth, is not the majestic, imperious queen of tragedy for whom Shakespeare's Antony deserted honor. She is frankly a wanton and at the end she repents of her waywardness and seeks to retrieve her fame by dying as befits an empress. The Chorus accentuates the moral; through licence, lust, and riot confusion entered into Egypt and caused the downfall of a mighty state. This patently virtuous treatment of the legend did not satisfy the anonymous Brandon. In his *Octavia* Cleopatra is deprived both of her glory and her beauty. Octavia holds the stage, reproving the indelicate expressions of the ladies attending her, praying for Antony's conversion, and exhorting Cæsar not to war on him for the sake of revenge. Fortunately for Octavia the author never exhibits her with her rival, as Dryden dared to do—indeed Cleopatra never appears at all in Brandon's play. The work is one long pæon of praise for female virtue, designed, it would seem, not as a supplement to Daniel's play as some commentators suggest, but rather in answer to it.

The remaining tragedies of Daniel, Greville, and Alexander discuss in a ventriloquizing fashion through dramatic puppets, the question of a sovereign's responsibility. All three men were friends of the great so their ideas are not alone the result of theorizing *a posteriori*. Daniel in dedicating his *Philotas* to the Prince promises that a perusal of the play will show how untrustworthy are the judgments of the mob, how men disguise their ends, and "plant bad courses under pleasing shewes." So precisely to the point did Daniel compose his dramatic treatise on statecraft that he found himself enmeshed in the Essex affair, although a modern eye can see little in the story of the Macedonian conspirator who finally suffered death for his indiscreet words about "the yong man" Alexander, which could trouble even so vigilant an intelligence service as that maintained by Elizabeth's ministers.

Greville's tragedies are really his *Treatises of Monarchies* expanded in dramatic form. His own words about his purpose in writing them deserve quoting for the illumination they give to contemporary theories of tragedy:

> Now to return to the Tragedies remaining, my purpose in them was, not (with the Ancient) to exemplifie the disastrous miseries of mans life, where Order, Lawes, Doctrine, and Authority are unable to protect Innocency from the exorbitant wickedness of power, and so out of that melancholike Vision, stir horrour, or murmur against Divine Providence: nor yet (with the Modern) to point out Gods revenging aspect upon every particular sin, to the despaire, or confusion of mortality; but rather to trace out the high waies of ambitious Governours . . . . Againe for the Arguments of these Tragedies they be not naked, and casuall, like the Greeke, and Latine, nor (I confesse) contrived with the variety, and un-expected encounters of the Italians, but nearer Level'd to those humours, councels, and practices, wherein I thought fitter to hold the attention of the Reader, than in the strangeness, or perplexedness of witty Fictions. . . . . [37]

The ethic of *Mustapha* and *Alaham* is Stoic and Calvinistic.[38] Man is naturally depraved; to struggle against the fate allotted him is useless. Even the characters which seem to us virtuous because they dare resist tyranny receive the evident censure of the author. In *Alaham* even the form is affected by the theme of the tragedy. Greville abandons the typical figures of the Senecan chorus—old men and women, counsellors—and introduces in their place morality figures, after the first act Good Spirits, after the second Furies, Malice, Craft, Pride, Corrupt Reason and Evil Spirits, after the third act a dialogue between the Good and Evil Spirits.

The tragedies of the northern lord, Alexander of Stirling, least of all among the closet dramas deserve the name dramatic. The story of Croesus, for instance, falls into three sections, each completely dis-sociated from the other two. At Croesus' invitation Solon visits his court. The extravagance and shallowness of life there is too much for the straight-laced philosopher. He speaks his mind and is sent packing. In the third act begins the story of the death in a boar hunt of Croesus' favorite son, Atis. When this theme is exhausted, the author proceeds with an account of the defeat and humiliation of the

---

[37] *Life of Sidney,* pp. 221-223.

[38] Professor Croll discusses the morality of the plays in his *The Works of Fulke Greville,* Philadelphia, 1903, pp. 42-43.

proud Croesus at the hands of the Persians. Though the plot has no unity, the tone of the piece, set by the chorus, is conventionally Stoic. One encounters the usual aphorisms about the fraility and uselessness of life, the worth of virtue, the controlling power of fate over man's destiny. The total impression sought by the author can be sur-mized from some lines of the final chorus:

> Is't not a wonder thus to see
>   How by experience each man reeds
> In practis'd volumes penn'd by deeds,
>   How things below inconstant be;
> Yet whil'st our selves continue free,
>   We ponder oft, but not apply
> That pretious oyle, which we might buy,
>   Best with the price of others paines.[39]

The remaining three dramas, *Darius, The Alexandrean Tragedy, Julius Cæsar,* dwell upon the woes of monarchs and the folly of their pride. It is odd that some researching student hunting sources for the *Cotter's Saturday Night* has not pillaged the last chorus of the *Darius:*

> O happie he who farre from ·Fame at home,
> Securely sitting by a quiet fire,
> (Though having little) doth no more desire,
> But first himselfe, then all things doth o'ercome.[40]

That Alexander's motive in writing these "Tragicall Poems" was the orthodox Renaissance one of Horatian origin, may be gathered from a sentence in the preface to the Reader in the 1603 edition of the *Darius.* He asks for sparing and courteous censure of his faults, "for that the imperfection of the worke is supplied with the worthiness of the matter, and with an earnest desire of procuring thereby thy pro-fite and delite."

Just at the turn of the century the Elizabethans were presented by Shakespeare with the greatest of all revenge plays, *Hamlet.* The old horrors of the popular Seneca have become in it so transmuted that few who read it now are aware of the melodramatic plot which gives it form. Seneca, the moralist, whose Stoic utterances had been drowned in the shrieks and tears of the victims of his English imitators, is heard no Seneca, the moralist, whose Stoic utterances had been drowned in the play's philosophy but in much of its atmosphere and action, is in part

[39] *Poetical Works of Sir William Alexander,* ed. by Kastner and Charlton, Vol. I, p. 109, ll. 2889-2896.
[40] *Ibid.,* p. 288, ll. 2195-2198.

responsible for one of the sublimest ethical dramas the world possesses. Moral Seneca lives on in the works just described or in the gentle essays of men like Sir William Cornwallis, who at approximately the time in which Hamlet appeared, put forth his *Discourses upon Seneca the Tragedian* (1601). From a series of golden texts, drawn from the tragedies, Sir William builds up a volume of stale Stoic-Christian comment on statecraft and religion, fame and prosperity, happiness and adversity, using the same Seneca who, probably quite unknown to the essayist, had indirectly inspired a great poet to produce something new under the sun. The contrast is striking. The early Senecans had imitated his tragedies or at least praised them because they contained instructive matter. Shakespeare employs what many men would have considered the dross from which the gold was to be extracted—the horrors and the terrors—and makes a drama which has since been held the most precious literary possession of the English race.

III

THE PROFESSIONAL PLAYWRIGHTS AND MORALITY

In the third decade of Elizabeth's reign the writing of plays became a profession. The scanty evidence concerning the lives of earlier dramatists shows them to have been a motley company composed largely of ministers and schoolmasters with a few men, like Gosson and Munday, in their midst, who were dependent for a livelihood, to some extent at least, on the product of their pens.[1] However much these amateur playwrights differed in social position or literary skill they agreed in proposing that the stage should supplement the teaching of the pulpit. As the preceding chapters show, didacticism as a function of the drama is equally evident in the Senecan plays produced by the courtiers at the Law Inns and in the late Tudor moralities based on social dogmas and played before the vulgar audiences in the inn yards of London and provincial cities.

The significance of the emergence in the 1580's of a group of professional playwrights who at once took the place of their amateur predecessors and the sudden elevation of the art of writing plays to a professional status is perhaps not fully apparent at first thought. It meant, as one can see readily enough, that the theater was now of such importance in Elizabethan society that writers might hope to make a living by furnishing plays for the newly formed dramatic companies. It meant further the beginning of what, for lack of a better phrase, may be called the professional attitude as distinguished from the earlier universally didactic attitude toward the business of playmaking. Plays henceforth were constructed with care, provided with the best poetry

[1] Lewis Wager, author of *The Life and Repentance of Mary Magdalene*, was rector of St. James Garlickhithe after March 28, 1560. Woodes, who wrote *The Conflict of Conscience*, had a congregation in the center of the Puritan district, Norwich. Edwardes and Udall were schoolmasters as for that matter was Lyly, the first of the professional playwrights. Whetstone, like Gascoigne, was attacked by his conscience after a period of riotous living and turned to literature to find a way of expiating his sins. Gosson and Munday were moved to repudiate their dramatic activities although the latter about 1580 "changed his copy and turned himself like the dog to his vomit, to plays again," and became, so Meres says, one of the "best for plotting" that England, even in the heyday of Shakespeare could boast.

and prose the author could command, and above all, they were nicely calculated to the public taste. No longer did the dramatist take great pains to tell his audience how they should receive his play, what good might come to them by following its admonitions. The old-fashioned didactic apology is almost entirely absent from the prologues and epilogues of the plays written by the University Wits. The exhortation to the audience to learn goodness from the spectacle of evil is replaced by a plea for "plaudites." Such plays as found favor were imitated year after year.

One would be bold to say, however, that the predecessors of Shakespeare thought it desirable or even possible to violate in their plays the accepted moral code of the day. Marlowe, the most radical of them all, was particularly careful to make his dramas conform in all essentials to traditional ethical standards. In their personal lives some of these professional dramatists showed little regard for the conventions of middle class morality. Their actions amounted to a public scandal. Their profligate ways furnished anecdotes for the sermons of Puritan ministers. But without exception their plays contradict their lives. Like Solness, the Master-builder, they could build higher than they could climb.

The case of Christopher Marlowe must be considered first, because he was both the greatest artist among his contemporaries and the most powerful influence in the group of young men of letters who arrived in London about 1585. He is a typical product of his age. That desirable quality, *virtu*, which the Italian Renaissance held necessary to greatness, the Herculean force which enables a man to snap the chains of circumstance which bind him, he possessed to a degree. He began life as a shoe-maker's son. He passed out of it the acknowledged leader of his profession and the friend of the powerful and great, in particular, Thomas Walsingham, cousin to the Queen's secretary, and Sir Walter Raleigh. The fame which was his he had forced Providence to yield him. Such a figure is naturally fascinating. Reading more in the plays than they legitimately may and conjecturing on the still baffling facts of his life, commentators have built up a kind of Marlowe myth which probably has some fanciful truth as regards the man but which finds little support from a close scrutiny of the plays. If they really are as unqualifiedly atheistic and unmoral as some historians appear to believe, they could never have received acclaim at a time when the Elizabethan theater was a genuinely popular institution. It will be useful to review briefly, before considering the morality of the dramas, what is actually known concerning the morals of the man.

The social historian who attempts to deduce the moral code of a period finds he is generally defining the undefinable. Only during times of great social homogeneity is such definition possible, although even then the accepted code is bound to be an ideal not completely realized. The Elizabethan age is notable as a period of transition during which entire classes of society were made over by the influx of new philosophies from the continent and the political and mercantile progress of the whole nation. But in one particular it is safe to say what the norm of conduct was. Elizabeth had determined the kind of *religion* which would best serve the interests of a new England. Endowed by Parliament with comprehensive power for the establishment of that religion she set about forcing conformity on all her people. An elaborate spy system made life highly dangerous for the Roman clergy and laity. With the "godly" sect she frequently dealt in person. Her finest exhibitions of temper were reserved for the bishops who permitted the scandalous "prophesyings" in their sees. Through all the growing discontent of the later years of her reign, with plots closing round her, she never relaxed her grip. About 1590 a new foe to the established order appeared—Deism. The Privy Council prosecuted the offenders with unrelenting zeal.

Marlowe at the time of his spectacular death was giving "his daily attendance" before a magistrate pending the disposition of charges of blasphemy and atheism made against him. It is doubtful if he could have cleared himself. Kyd had accused him and one Baines had supported the charges with monstrous allegations which would prove him a blasphemer, atheist, perhaps even a Sodomite and a traitor.[2] The Privy Council, harassed by Jesuits, Puritans, and Free-thinkers, was not inclined to examine evidence too carefully or consider motives.[3] Perhaps it was well for Marlowe that Francis Frizer got the upper hand in the tavern brawl which Mr. Hotson's discoveries have at last explained.

One is forced to conclude that Marlowe was a Free-thinker even though the extravagant charges of Baines look suspiciously like state's

[2] Marlowe, so he said, had declared he has as much right to coin money as the Queen herself.

[3] In the month of Marlowe's arrest (May 1593) they were concerned with libels "set upon the wal of the Dutch churchyard" which led to the search in Kyd's lodgings and to Marlowe's difficulties. On May 14 the "Maiour of Nottinham and his bretheren" reported "the lewd and unreverent words of one Isaac Rotheram." Isaac was indicted and rested in prison awaiting the action of the Assizes. On May 23 unreverent speeches of one Richard Danvers in Reading were considered, the information having come through a letter sent to the Archbishop of Canterbury and turned over to them for action. (Acts of the Privy Council for the year 1593.)

evidence.[4] The fragmentary brochure containing Deistic arguments found among Kyd's papers and claimed by him to be Marlowe's, with Kyd's twice-repeated allegations, and Greene's testimony contained in the *Groatsworth of Wit Bought with a Million of Repentance,* together with the unmistakable note of the plays, however cleverly muffled by the shrewdness of their author, make such a conclusion inevitable. But

[4] It may be well to list here the various scattered articles which bear in general on the subject of atheism in the reign of Elizabeth and in particular on Marlowe's case.

F. S. Boas in his edition of Kyd prints some of the documents, including Kyd's letter to Puckering denying the charges against him and implicating Marlowe, the fragment of the "theological disputation," and Baines' note accusing Marlowe of blasphemy. (In part only.)

M. Danclin in the *Revue Germanique,* 1913, 567ff., publishes in their entirety the following series of documents relating to atheism in high places:

1. "The theological disputation."

2. Baines' scurrilous denunciation of Marlowe.

3. Kyd's letter to Puckering.

4a. "Remembraunces of wordes and matter against Ric(hard) Cholmeley" in which he mentions Marlowe's having read his "atheist lecture" to Sir Walter Raleigh.

4b. "Ye athisme of Ch(olmeley) & others."

5. Letter reporting the capture of Cholmeley.

6. "Interrogatory to be ministered unto such as ar to be examined in her Majesty's name by vertue of Her Highness Commission for cawses ecclesiasticall." With this are depositions made by various persons, etc., in answer to these queries. Among these is an account of the dinner at Sir George Treuehard's where Raleigh argued with Ralph Ironside, minister of Winterbro, over the nature of the soul.

7. F. S. Boas, "New Light on Marlowe and Kyd," *Fortnightly Review,* 1899, pp. 222ff. (Mostly incorporated in his edition of Kyd and in Brie's article.)

8. Friedrich Brie, "Deismus u. Atheismus in der Englischen Renaissance," *Anglia,* Vol. 48. Discusses the problem in general and as it concerns Marlowe, Nash, Greene, and Raleigh.

9. C. F. Tucker Brooke, "The Reputation of Christopher Marlowe," *Conn. Acad. of Arts and Sciences, Transactions,* Vol. xxv, Art. V.

10. Ford K. Brown, "A Letter of Kyd's concerning Marlowe," *Litt. Supplement to the Times,* June 2, 1921. This document (Harl. MS. 6484f. 154) is apparently a second letter from Kyd to Lord Keeper Puckering, written, however, after Marlowe's death and substantiating Baines' charges of extreme and blasphemous atheism.

11. J. Leslie Hotson, *The Death of Christopher Marlowe,* 1925. In addition to his discoveries which illuminate the circumstances of Marlowe's death, Mr. Hotson publishes a *Certificate from the Privy Council in Favour of Marlowe* proving that in 1587, at least, the poet possessed the full confidence of that body.

there is another side to the story. Deism in 1590 was a fashionable vice, which in the next century was indulged in publicly by so influential a man as the ambassador to France, Sir Edward Herbert of Cherbury. During Elizabeth's regime it was necessarily quiescent, confined to a small group of "advanced" thinkers who discussed religion over their dinners and perhaps read "atheist lectures" to one another as Marlowe is reported to have done to Raleigh. When instances of blasphemy were brought to the attention of the Council they were bound to act, especially if the defendant lacked powerful supporters. But Raleigh who seems to have been at the center of a "school of atheism" apparently got free from the toils of the law without great difficulty though during the remainder of his life and even after his death statements of his unorthodoxy reappeared. Expediency governed Elizabeth's policy, and Raleigh was necessary to England in 1593. And so had Marlowe been in 1587. In that year the Council directed the University of Cambridge to give him his degree which was being withheld because of his frequent absences during the previous year.[5] The letter discloses the fact that Marlowe had been engaged in secret missions "in matters touching the benefit of his Countrie." (Hunting out Papists?) Whether the Lord Archbishop, the Lord Chancellor, the Lord Treasurer, the Lord Chamberlain, and Mr. Comptroller would have remembered this letter of theirs at Marlowe's trial in 1593 might well depend on his usefulness to the government and the political power of his patrons. Defenceless he would have been hanged; protected he might have escaped.

The Marlowe of the atheistical pamphlet could never have succeeded as a playwright. It is Marlowe the artist, able to accommodate himself to his age, thoroughly conscious of the exigencies of his art, who wrote the plays. Even as astute a critic as Symonds failed to understand this. In discussing the final scene in *Faustus* he wrote: "In depicting his end thus, with force so penetrative of imagination, did he mean to paint the terrors of his own remorseful soul; or, with an artist's irony, did he sacrifice the finest point of the situation to the conventions . . . . of accepted beliefs? This we cannot now decide. But the whole handling by Marlowe of the Faust-legend inclines one rather to believe that, if it is in any sense autobiographical, the poet was but an ill-contented and heart-sick atheist."[6] "Sacrifice to convention" is precisely what he did

[5] Hotson's *Death of Christopher Marlowe*, pp. 57ff.
[6] *Shakespeare's Predecessors*, p. 648 (edition of 1884).

in Faustus as in other instances where he encounters the dogma of the
Christian religion. Marlowe in his dramas holds the middle of the road
in religious matters as Elizabeth taught and required her subjects to do.
He expresses contempt for both Romanist and Puritan. Faustus bids
Mephistopheles return in the habit of a Franciscan: "That holy shape
becomes a divell best." (F. 260-261.) The friars in the *Jew of Malta*
violate the secret of the confessional, try to persuade the "converted"
Jew to dower their houses, and act in general in a fashion certain to
be pleasing to a Jesuit-baiting audience. The whole tone of the *Mas-
sacre at Paris* is naturally violently anti-Catholic. Now glance at the
other side. Wagner says (*Faustus* 220), "I will set my countenance like
a precisian." There is ridicule of the Puritan mode of swearing in the
speech of Pride (728).[7] It is true that Marlowe delights in slurring
Christians who do not keep faith. Barabas says of them:

> It's no sinne to deceive a Christian;
> For they themselves hold it a precinciple,
> Faith is not to be held with Heretickes;
> But all are Heretickes that are not Jewes. (*J. of M*. 1074-1077.)

Similar utterances on the part of Shylock have always been considered
an excellent observance of Horatian decorum on the part of their author.
In *Tamburlaine II* the Emperor Sigismund—a Catholic ruler be it
noted—confirms an oath with Orcanes of Natolia, solemnly swearing by
the "sonne of God and issue of a Mayd, sweet Jesus Christ" (2456ff.).
This troth he subsequently breaks through the instigation of Frederick
of Bohemia. Orcanes calls down God's vengeance on him:

> Thou Christ that art esteem'd omnipotent
> If thou wilt prove thyselfe a perfect God. . . . .
> Be now reveng'd upon this Traitor's soule. (2912-2914)

Justice by ordeal of battle falls on the traitor and the heathen Orcanes
raises thanks to Christ for the victory:

> Yet in my thoughts shall Christ be honoured
> Not dooing Mahomet an injurie,
> Whose power had share in this our victory. . . . . (2954-2956)

The splitter of hairs may find an exquisite irony in Marlowe's treatment
of this situation but his audience would scarcely have penetrated beyond
the evident facts: a Catholic king breaks troth; the other party to the
oath, though a Mahometan, challenges Christ to punish the troth-

---

[7] See page 70 in H. Logeman's *Faustus-notes*, Gand 1898, for a note on the
satire of the Puritans in this play.

breaker, which is promptly done and the fact acknowledged by the
heathen victor.

But this is negative proof.   Does Marlowe anywhere speak well
of Christians and not always ill of Romanists, Puritans and Christian
troth-breakers?   Once, at least, he does something like that.   In *Tamburlaine I* he uses the magnanimity of his hero toward the Christian
captives kept as slaves by the Turks to make him more just in the eyes
of his audience:

> *Tamb.*   I that am tearm'd the Scourge and Wrath of God,
> The only feare and terrour of the world,
> Wil first subdue the Turke, and then inlarge
> Those Christian Captives, which you keep as slaves,
> Burdening their bodies with your heavie chaines,
> And feeding them with thin and slender fare,
> That naked rowe about the Terrene sea. . . . . (1142-1158)

While the discussion is centered on Tamburlaine, it may be well
to settle a difficult problem in connection with the two plays to which
he gives his name.   How can it be, one wonders, that a hero so ruth-
less, so utterly lacking in the Christian virtues of love, humility, and
mercy, a character expressly conceived of as representing in the extreme
the Italian quality of *virtu,* how can it be that such a hero was not only
tolerated but applauded ceaselessly on the Elizabethan stage?   The
answer lies in the traditional, mythical Tamburlaine which Marlowe
dramatized.   Sixteenth century readers long before Marlowe wrote his
two-part play were interested in the Scythian shepherd and had learned
to make excuses for his monstrous conduct.   In 1571 Thomas Fortescue published *The Forest,* the 14th chapter of which contains a long
account of Tamburlaine's life derived from Mexia's *Silva de varia lecion*
(1543).   The whole tone of the chapter is apologetic toward the hero's
cruelties and makes much of the popular belief that he was actually the
Scourge of God, Divine Wrath made manifest on earth.   "But it is to
be supposed that god stirred hym uppe an instrument, to chastice these
proud and wicked nations."   To strengthen this argument which, if
accepted would of course excuse any nation wanton cruelty on the part
of the Scourge, Fortescue recounts a story told by Pope Pius, "which
lived in his tyme, or at least eight or tenne yeres after hym," concerning his merciless treatment of women and children sent out to him on
the third day of a certain siege:

"A certaine Marchaunte of Genua was then in his campe, who had often
recourse to him, who also used hym in causes familiarly and who for this

facte seemed verie bloodie and barbarous, hardned hymselfe to demaunde hym
the cause why he used theim so cruelly considering thei yelded themselves, crav-
ing grace and pardon: to whom he answered in most furious wrath and yre,
his face redde and firie, his eyes all flamunge with burnyng spearckles, as it
were blasing out, on everie side. Thou supposest me to be a man but thou
to muche abbusest me, for none other am I but the wrathe and vengeaunce
of God and ruine of the worlde. . . . ."[8]

Whetstone in the *Heptameron of Civil Discourses* (16th day) gives
Tamburlaine a good character.[9] Ismarrito is described by him reading
"The rare Historie of Tamburlaine the Great, surnamed Flagellum Dei,
where he much admired the vertues of the man, who of a labouring
Pesaunt . . . . by his vertues and invincible valure became a great
Monarch." Robert Greene in a casual reference in his *Mamillia* apolo-
gizes for his conduct: "Prince Tamburlaine, the most bloody butcher
in the world, never shed blood, where there was submission."[10] It is
of course proper to question whether the conception of Tamburlaine
as the Flagellum Dei was widespread or whether, indeed, his fame
was general before Marlowe. Additional evidence is available in the
popularity of Thomas Newton's *History of the Saracens* (1575) which
contains a supplementary account of Tamburlaine. Collier says of it:
"The rapid progress the Turks had made in Europe, previous to the
battle of Lepanto in 1571, gave great attraction to Newton's production. . . . ."[11] It would appear, then, that Marlowe's success in his first
play was due, in part at least, to the fact that he was giving concrete
form to the legend about a hero already worthy in the eyes
of his audience because they held him to be the incarnation of God's
wrath visited upon the stubborn and perverse heathen.[12]

Any Elizabethan whose scruples would permit his witnessing a moral-

[8] A. Wagner, *Tamburlaine,* Heilbronn, 1885, xix-xx passim.

[9] Published 1582.

[10] Grosart edition, II, p. 81.

[11] J. P. Collier, *Biographical and Critical Account of the Rarest Books in
the English Language,* 1865, vol. II, p. 30.

[12] Criticism like the following (Herford, *Social History of the English Drama,*
p. 51) is worthless in view of these facts: "It is characteristic of the man and
of the age that no Nemesis is felt to impend over his boundless arrogance; the
Elizabethan character was too thoroughly steeped in it to permit of the religious
horror which it aroused in the Greek. Tamburlaine does not fall; his death by
disease has no moral significance; it is the extinction of a glorious comet in
mid-career; and his son is crowned at his death bed that he may continue a
work which is only interrupted, not destroyed and perpetuate a spirit withdrawn
by the stroke of a fate in which there is no suggestion of retribution."

ity play could have endured *The tragicall History of Doctor Faustus* without any sense of wrong-doing for it is actually a morality itself. The final chorus speaks a word of admonition even as the epilogues of the moral interludes were wont to do and the fundamental conception— the warfare between the Vices and the Virtues for the possession of man's soul—is a theme as old in English drama as the *Castle of Perseverance.* Marlowe even goes so far as to introduce the Good and Evil Angels, characters not supplied by the Faust-book which is otherwise his source.[13] The similarity between *Faustus* and Nathaniel Woodes' *Conflict of Conscience,* a popular controversial morality of the 1580's, has been noted by Miss Spens and Mr. Mackenzie. Both plays are based on well-known stories of contemporary events. In both a learned man falls into sin and is kept in his wretched state by sensual pleasure and his belief that he is so far sunk in sin that escape from damnation is impossible.[14] The chief difference between the two plays appears in the conclusion. Woodes' Philologus is saved from suicide and after thirty weeks of suffering returns to the fold. Faustus, as the legend demands, dies with his guilt upon him. In early Tudor days such a conclusion would have been scarcely moral but, as instances in Chapter I show, by 1580 the sinners are frequently permitted to die, unredeemed. This is true of *The Longer Thou Livest, Enough is as good as a Feast*, and Gascoigne's *Glass of Government.* In *Like Will to Like* the feeble Virtues prove quite incapable of turning the rogues from their vice and preventing this just punishment. So far from being what Symonds thought likely, the autobiographical record of the sufferings of a heart-sick atheist, *Faustus* is really a remarkable example of what genius can do with convention. Working with materials frayed by years of use but dear to his audience, Marlowe unconsciously produced a drama toward which generations of morality-writers had

[13] The English Faust-book survives in no edition earlier than 1592. But the title-page implies previous publication, viz., "Newly imprinted and in convenient places imperfect matter amended." Discussion in Logeman, xiv-xv.

[14] The Faust-book makes much of this powerlessness of the guilty man to shake off the sense of guilt and hope for redemption: "Doctor Faustus was ever pondering with himselfe how he might get loose from so damnable an end as he had given himself unto, both of body and soule: but as his repentaunce was like to that of Cain and Judas, he thought his sinnes greater than God could forgive, hereupon rested his minde: he looked up to heaven, but sawe nothing therein; for his heart was so possessed with the Divel that hee coulde thinke of nought els but hell, and the paynes thereof." Logeman edition, p. 25.

been groping. *Faustus* stands at the end of a tradition. Through it a host of inglorious Woodeses and Wagers speak their hearts.[15]

As regards religion, Marlowe is evidently orthodox in his dramas. His heroes may now and again speak atheism but they do so in accord with decorum since they are Jews or heathen. The cruel Tamburlaine is allowed to die unpunished, but what moral necessity is there for punishing the Scourge of God? The blasphemous Jew falls into his own trap and perishes miserably; the Duke of Guise, champion of the Catholic cause dies with *Vive la messa* on his lips but dies, nevertheless, in expiation of his sins. Faustus' final agony is inevitable from the opening scenes.

Any further discussion of Marlowe's acceptance or defiance of particular moral conventions belongs properly to later chapters, but passing mention must be made of his attitude toward women. The ideal Elizabethan woman is chaste, loyal, obedient and patient under injustice. Frequently her influence regenerates the man she loves. Zenocrate is such a woman. She shrinks at first from the passion and brutality of Tamburlaine but once cognizant of his virtues and certain of being made an honest woman by him, she becomes his loyal and obedient helpmeet. During the siege of Damascus she prays for his soul, that heaven may not punish his vindictiveness. For her dear sake he saves her father's life. And at the end, about to make her queen of Persia, he removes suspicion of unhonesty from her name.

> And for all blot of foule unchastity,
> I record heaven, her heavenly selfe is cleare. . . . . (2268-2269)

The domestic life of the Scythian conqueror is above reproach. Queen Isabella, wife to Edward II, remains loyal to her husband beyond all reasonable demand. Her eventual act of treason lodges her in the tower to await trial for murder. Abigail in *The Jew of Malta* is placed in a difficult position for a girl whom the author intends shall act morally. She very properly deserts her father when his hideous criminality culminates in the deaths of Lodovico and Mathias. But she will not betray him to his enemies.

> . . . . Oh Barabas,
> Though thou deservest hardly at my hands,
> Yet never shall these lips bewray thy life. (1298-1300)

[15] I was delighted to discover some time after writing the above that Professor Schücking in his *Character Problems in Shakespeare's Plays* looks upon Faustus as a conventional drama the limits of which tradition dictated.

The story of Pilia Borza and the Courtesan which ends with their deaths in the fourth act of *The Jew* shows Marlowe meting out punishment to the "bad woman" as his contemporaries all did. She was a sinner and there's an end on it; sentimentalizing over her misfortune would not accord with the prevailing attitude toward viciousness.

Only once—at the end of *Faustus*—does Marlowe range himself with his predecessors who urge their plays upon their auditors for the moral lesson to be found in them. But it is plain he knew well enough that a successful dramatist cannot outrage the social conventions of his time. Yet this need not lessen our appreciation of his greatness. Marlowe was essentially a technician, conscious of the reform he had wrought in the history of play making. And he was a great poet searching the heart for new secrets. Men like him seldom, if ever, are interested in remaking the moral code.

It is an odd fact that the one other predecessor of Shakespeare who was to have an influence on him equal to Marlowe's should have been a man so dissimilar in every way to the "atheist" and blasphemer. John Lyly's personal life seems to have been impeccable, as schoolmasters' lives are bound to be. As early as 1579 he raised his voice against the sin of free-thinking which, if we may believe the implication of the conversation between Euphues and Atheos, infested Oxford and other learned centers.[16] By way of introducing this moral dialogue between a believer and an atheist, he offers it to the "Gentleman Schollers of Athens" as a "touchstone where unto everye one ought to trust and by whiche everye one shoulde try himselfe. . . . . " From such a defender of established religion whose words, though nicely poised and balanced, ring with a quality like those of Ascham and Stubbes, one might have expected violently moral dramas. But Lyly's plays are really set in the land of gallantry which Charles Lamb wrongly imagined the home of Restoration drama. They are beautiful and bloodless. One may as well seek for the solution of ethical problems in *A Midsummer Night's Dream* as in *Campaspe* and *Gallathea*. Only occasionally does any note of passion or feeling sound, e.g., when Diogenes rails at the Athenians and in the remorseful speeches of Midas, and even there observance of decorum requires semblance of emotion.[17] Lyly quite definitely considered the function of the drama the entertainment of the spectators; he wished to move "inward delight and soft smiling." And yet he is

[16] R. W. Bond, *The Complete Works of John Lyly*, Vol. I, pp. 301-305.

[17] *Campaspe*, IV-1; *Midas*, III-1.

no countenancer of the particular kind of loose speech which moderns
find objectionable in the plays of his contemporaries. Only occasionally
does the slant-eyed joke slip out of the dialogues of his pages or courtiers.[18] Several of the prologues introduce the Horatian precept: *Aut
prodesse volunt, aut delectare poetae.* Thus the actor spoke for his
company at the Blackfriars' performance of *Campaspe:* "But how-
soever we finish our worke we crave pardon, if we offend in matter, and
patience if we transgresse in manners. We have mixed mirth with
counsell, and discipline with delight, thinking it not amisse in the same
garden to sowe pot-hearbes, that we set flowers." The prologue to
Sapho and Phao is written in similar vein. In the prologue to *Gallathea*
Lyly turns the usual apology into a graceful compliment to the queen.
"So have we endevoured with all care, that what wee present your
Highness shoulde neyther offend in Scaene nor sillable, knowing that
as in the ground where Gold groweth, nothing will prosper but Golde,
so in your Maiestes minde, where nothing doth harbor but vertue, nothing can enter but vertue." Yet in spite of these pretentions of a didactic
purpose Lyly's view of the function of the drama approaches a purely
aesthetic theory.[19] His position in this particular is unique among
Shakespeare's predecessors. No other dramatist before Marston follows his example.

The Victorian enthusiasts for the Elizabethan drama dropped silent
tears over the fate of Robert Greene. The "new" psychologists would
see in him an interesting form of the religious complex. In spite of
his dissolute life—and his admirers cannot deny that fact—his mind
dwelt as much upon repentance as John Milton's pondered the problem
of temptation. Toward the end of his life it became the central theme
of his writing and he himself repented so often and so extrava-
gantly during his last hours that one would be inclined to question
his sincerity if public contrition were not a recognized symptom of such
mental illness.

Playwriting seems to have been scarcely more than an episode in
Greene's busy journalistic life. If the chronology established by Gay-

[18] *Gallathea,* Vol. II, pp. 462-3; *Midas* Vol. III, p. 120; *Mother Bombie,*
Vol. III, p. 204. (References are to pages in Bond's edition.)

[19] He styles *Endimion* but "a tale of the Man in the Moone." *The Woman
in the Moon* is a "Poets dreame." The Prologue at the Court presenting *Campaspe*
wishes the play may be "thought the daunsing of Agrippa his shadowes. . . . .
With us it is like to fare, as with these torches, which giving light to others,
consume themselves; and we shewing delight to others, shame ourselves."

ley and Dickinson be right, the dramas belong in the middle of his
career, with the amorous stories preceding and the low-life pamphlets
following.[20]   His plays in almost every instance are derivative.   Unlike
Marlowe he does not seem to have been a conscious innovator.   That
he discovered the type known as Romantic Comedy was a happy
consequence of his previous experience as a writer of romances done
in English after the Italian manner.

From such a popular author conformity in matters of religion and
morality is to be expected.   To an even greater extent than Marlowe
he concedes to the universal demand that the theater instruct in virtue
or, at least, that it discountenance evil.   In his *Never too Late* written,
it is true, after his famous conversion but at the height of his dramatic
career, Greene through the mouth of his Palmer gives his judgment of
"Playes, Playmakers and Players."   In the beginning at Athens and
Rome plays taught morality.   "To be short, Lecherie, Covetousness,
Pride, self-love, disobedience of parents, and such vices predominant
both in age and youth were shot at, not only with examples, and instances to feede the eye but with golden sentences of morrall words
to please the care. . . . ."   Then came a decline when covetous men made
money from the profession.   "Thus sir, have you heard my opinion
briefly of plaies, that Menander devised them for the suppressing of
vanities, necessarie in a commonwealth, as long as they are used in
their right kind. . . . ."[21]

How far does Greene's own dramatic writing conform to Menander's requirements?   There is first the evidence of *A Looking Glass for
London and England*—a play done in collaboration with Lodge—the
only professedly moral play written by the wits.[22]   As has already
been remarked (Chapter I) the spectacle was probably relished chiefly
for its amazing variety of incident and the intentionally spectacular

[20] Churton Collins dissents in important particulars.   He places *A Looking
Glass* as late as 1590 but he agrees in the main with the accepted chronology
which makes Greene's dramatic career extend from 1587-1591.

[21] This discussion of plays may be found in Grosart's edition of the works
of Greene, Vol. VIII, pp. 128-134.

[22] It makes little difference in this connexion how the division of labor between
the co-authors is decided.   The tone of the play never changes.   The speeches
of Oseas and Jonah might almost be exchanged.   The sinfulness in high life
is paralleled by the injustice and cruelty manifest among the characters of the
sub-plots.   All the sinners make some sort of restitution at the end.   The division
of scenes is most fully discussed by Gayley in his *Representative English Comedies*,
vol. I, p. 405.

treatment of the scenes of debauchery at court. But the didactic purpose, visibly represented by the speeches of the two prophets is evident at the end of nearly every scene. In one other place Greene definitely becomes the preacher and moralizes his song. The fourth scene of the fifth act of *James IV* appears to be a gratuitous discussion of the unhealthy state of the kingdom on the part of a Lawyer, a Merchant and a Divine. Through their cross-accusations a lamentable state of corruption and moral indifference is exposed, quite without relevance to the rest of the play.[23] There are reminiscences, in the Chorus speeches of Bohan in the same play, of the old-fashioned didactic address of the moral prologue. The tirades of the Bishop of St. Andrews likewise point the moral and serve to direct the understanding of the audience.

We have already found Marlowe willing to conform in his plays to the religious prejudice of his audience. Greene follows his example. A spectacular instance occurs in the fourth act of *Alphonsus*. Mahomet, through the Brazen-head, prophesies a victory for the Turks. Nevertheless Belinus who boasts that God Mahound is on his side dies wretchedly and Amurack, the Great Turk, is obliged to capitulate. This incident reminds one of the more sensational scene in *Tamburlaine II*, 4290ff., in which the Alcoran is burned before the wide-eyed groundlings. Friar Bacon, after putting to shame the Great German necromancer, renounces his devilish art to spend the remnant of his life "in pure devotion," praying God for forgiveness. It would never do to allow so fascinating a sinner to die unredeemed.[24] And this repentance is, like that of other characters of Greene, a sudden and somewhat casual thing:

> Yet, Bacon, cheere thee, drowne not in despaire:
> Sinnes have their salves, repentance can do much,
> Thinke Mercie sits where Justice holds her seate. (End of Act IV)

The repentance motive appears in *Orlando*. The villain Sacripant when charged with deceiving Angelica's lover breaks forth with:

> O, that's the sting that pricks my conscience!
> Oh, that's the hell my thoughts abhore to thinke! (V. 1255-1256)

The Machiavellian parasite in *James IV* after his nefarious plans go wrong curses his kind and hides himself awaiting the judgment of

[23] Collins *(Plays and Poems of Robert Greene)* believes this scene is by Greene though possibly an interpolation from some other play. Dickinson expresses doubt.

[24] Greene is, of course, following the account of Bacon's life which was his source.

God upon him. The depths of woe of James are profound. The ghosts of his slain subjects pursue him in his palace and on the field of battle. In the end, his contrition complete, he solemnly promises his royal father-in-law he will sin no more.

Whether from conviction or design Greene was evidently determined to bid for success as a moral dramatist. His singularly idealistic conception of womanhood, repeatedly and fancifully ascribed to a nostalgic memory of his own badly treated wife may more safely be regarded as a reflex of the popular lady-worship. What a virtuous company they make, these heroines of his! The heathen Iphigena, haughty toward the lusty conqueror of her father, reluctantly won by him and then only on assurance that she will be made an honest bride; the wronged but constant Angelica; Margaret of Fressingfield who repulses the amorous advances of a prince and chooses to be faithful to an honest lover, her devotion continuing under his own apparent faithlessness; and last of all the noble pair in *James IV*—a Countess who blushes at the name of lust, a Queen who can forgive even an attempt against her life. Marlowe contrived to make his Italianate heroes acceptable to English morality. Greene's heroines are English born and bred but their portraits have been painted by a master schooled in Italy. Margaret among her cream bowls shines like a lady in a sonnet. But the virtues of these ladies are English virtues, albeit their graces were acquired in the novels of Greene's Italian masters.

In his last days Greene renounced the sins of his youth, including among them his plays. Not content, as such penitents seldom are content, with saving only his own soul, he exhorted his companions in shame, Marlowe, Lodge, and Peele, to abandon their wickedness and follow his example.[25] There is bitterness of disappointment as well as terror of the night in this amazing document. Yet in spite of his self-accusation Greene remains the most moral, the most consciously didactic dramatist among the predecessors of Shakespeare.[26]

[25] The famous passage in *A Groatsworth of Wit*, Grosart XII, p. 142.

[26] Some of Greene's contemporaries speak of the moral worth of his productions. The third sonnet in *Greene's Funerals*, a posthumus defence of the dramatist, for instance, refers to him as follows:

> His gadding Muse, although it ran of love,
> Yet did hee sweetly moralize, his songs;
> Ne ever gave the looser cause to laugh,
> Ne men of Judgment for to be offended.

(Malone Society Reprint of the *Funerals*.)

Of the remaining members of this company there is little that need be said here. Peele stands far below Marlowe, Lyly, and Greene. He originated nothing except the dramatic burlesque and he was woefully lacking in the architectonic powers which his fellows possessed. His skill as a juggler of words—Nashe calls him *primus artifex verborum*—endeared him to an age intoxicated by the sound and fury of language. In questions of morality he conforms. In the story of David and Bethsabe he found ready at hand a tale of sin and repentance, and he misses no opportunity of making the sin as impressive as may be and the contrition spectacular.[27] The confession of vile Queen Elinor (*Edward I*, scene xxv) suggested in a stanza of the ballad which is the source of the play, testifies to the popularity of such last-hour exhibitions of penitence.[28] In the *Battle of Alcazar*, a play crowded with Senecan horrors—dumb shows, ghosts crying revenge, and bloody battles—Peele once touches religious prejudices.[29] The Irish Bishop in Act II, 2 comes in for some gentle abuse from Stukeley and Hercules. Yet in spite of this anti-Romanist by-play his Catholic Majesty of Portugal is represented as undertaking a war to aid the deposed Moor in good faith, hoping to advance the Kingdom of Christ.

Once only, and then appropriately enough in a play which looks backward—*David and Bethsabe*—does Peele assume the rôle of the arbiter of morals before his audience. He reverts to the use of the obsolescent "expositor" in the character of a Chorus figure. The pregnant words spoken by him at the end of Act II might belong in some Senecan play of the Law Inns:

> O dreadfull precedent of his just doom
> Whose holy heart is never toucht with ruth
> Of fickle beauty or of glorious shape
> But with the virtue of an upright soul,
> Humble and zealous in his inward thoughts
> Though in his person loathsome and deform'd.[30]

[27] Act II, 2 where David moved by Nathan's parable falls to the ground in loud lamentation.

[28] Compare the speeches of Ales in *Arden of Feversham* (V, 5) and Sanders' wife in *A Warning for Fair Women* (ll. 1644-1673).

[29] Any comments based on the present text of this play must be made with reservations for it is preserved in a wretched state. Mr. W. W. Greg believes the 1594 quarto to be an eviscerated copy prepared for a tour in the provinces. Ascription to Peele is, moreover, doubtful.

[30] Bullen's edition, vol. II, p. 72.

Both Lodge and Nashe, although they contributed little to the drama themselves, defended the stage with vigor and are, indeed, the chief opponents of the Puritans in the first skirmishes of their war against the players. Lodge appears as the co-author of the excessively moral *Looking Glass for London* and independently with *The Wounds of Civil War,* a tedious Roman history full of alarums and excursions. It is principally for his *Defence of Poetry,* written to "school" the schoolmaster Gosson that partisans of the drama are grateful to him. In the section devoted to the theater he advances the usual arguments of the humanists in its favor, commending the purity and high-mindedness of the classical dramatists. In one particular the defense is unusual; Lodge almost alone among contemporary defenders of the stage advances Tully's definition of comedy as an *"Imitatio vitae, speculum consuetudinis, atque imago veritatis."* He does not find English drama perfect but he hopes for a reformed stage and urges the magistrates to abolish abuses like Sunday playing. There was still some hope in those years of reconciling the Puritans and the players. In his *Wits Miserie and the Worlds Madness* Lodge cautions actors and authors against various indiscretions. "If they use no other mirth but Eutrapelian urbanitie, and pleasure mixed with honestie, it is to bee borne withall; but filthie speaking Scurrilitie, unfit for chast eares that I wish with the Apostle that it should not bee named amongst Christians. Againe in stage plaies to make use of Hystoricall Scripture, I hold with the Legists odious."[31] Mr. Thompson sees in three lines of his *Scillaes Metamorphosis* (1599) a renouncing of "what he had formerly so bravely defended."[32] But these lines,

> To write no more of that whence shame doth grow,
> Or tie my pen to Pennie-knaves delight,
> But live with fame, and so for fame to *wright.* . . . .[33]

have the look of the usual Elizabethan contempt for dramatic writing. Shakespeare wrote something to the same effect, one remembers, in the 110th sonnet.

Only two plays of Nashe survive—*Dido,* written in collaboration with Marlowe, and a kind of super-vaudeville piece, *Summer's Last Will and Testament. The Isle of Dogs* has unfortunately perished.

[31] Hunterian Club edition, p. 40. This remark is interesting in connexion with Lodge's own Biblical play, *The Looking Glass.*

[32] *Controversy between the Puritans and the Stage,* p. 78.

[33] Hunterian Club edition, p. 28.

The *Dido* is frankly pagan. *The Last Testament* for the most part avoids the grossness of Elizabethan low-comedy. A few passages must have annoyed the Puritans. Says Will, the Clown: "I promise you truly, I was almost asleep; I thought I had been at a Sermon."

The fatal breach between the theaters and the "godly sect" was made about 1590. Nashe helped to widen it. An active participant in the attack on Martin-Marprelate and a member of the group of playwrights discussed in this chapter, he and his kind henceforth became identified in the minds of the Puritans as the arch-foes of righteousness. His fine defence of the stage found in *Pierce Penniless* could hardly purge bitterness from the understandings of those it was intended to convert. Nor were such arguments as the following well calculated to win the pious: since the afternoon is the idle time of day when men about town will be "gameing, following of harlots, drinking, or seeing a play, is it not better . . . . that they should betake them to the least, which is playes? Nay, what if I prove playes to be no extreame, but a rare exercise of vertue?" First in their favor is the love of England which histories inspire. Next, in "playes, all coosonages, all cunning drifts overgylded with outward holinesse, all strategens of warre, all the canker-wormes that breede on the rust of peace, are most lively anatomiz'd; they shew the ill successe of treason, the fall of hastie climbers, the wretched ende of usurpers, the miserie of civill dissention, & howe just God is evermore in punishing of murther. . . . ."[34]

Who may say Nashe overstated the case? The plays of his contemporaries, as this chapter bears witness, were "souninge in moral vertu" although the Bohemians who wrote them were scarcely in a position themselves to recommend their pieces as correctives to vice. How does it happen, then, that a considerable part of the Elizabethan public had by 1590 repudiated the drama? The answer to this question will be essayed in the following pages.

[34] The defense is to be read in the Shakespeare Society's edition of *Pierce Penniless's Supplication to the Devil,* pp. 59-63.

IV

THE PURITANS

It may seem a superfluous matter to enter again upon a discussion of the controversy between the Puritans and the stage since the various aspects of the question have been thoroughly reviewed in the past.[1] My only excuse can be, and it seems a sufficient one, that those who review the problem have been content for the most part with a chronicle of events; an essay at an interpretation of them will not be unprofitable.

In the early days of Protestantism in England the drama was an ally of the new religion. We possess moralities—and these represent a larger number that have perished—written to satirize the abuses of the old religion and to defend the dogmas of the new. Consequently not until 1570 does any kind of determined opposition to the stage, based on moral arguments, appear in pamphlet or ordinance eminating from Puritan sources. Now it happens that during that decade the drama passed through a period of secularization, not completed until 1590, but nevertheless an immediate occasion of grave doubt to many serious-minded men.[2] They realized that the players were foisting something new on them and they were troubled. This new drama the author of the *Third Blast of Retrait from Plaies and Theatres* describes:

"The noblest lier is become the best poet . . . . our nature is led awaie with vanitie, which the auctor perceaving frames himself with novelties and strange trifles to content the vaine humours of his rude auditors, faining countries never heard of; monsters & prodigious creatures, that are not, as of the Arimaspie, or the Grips, the Pigmies, the Cranes & other such notorious lies. And if they

---

[1] The documents are analyzed and some attempt at a conclusion is made by Mr. E. N. S. Thompson, *The Controversy between the Puritans and the Stage*. The opposition of the City officials Dean Gildersleeve treated definitively. Mr. Symmes considers the controversy in its relation to the development of dramatic criticism in Chap. IV; also V and VI *passim*. Practically the only interpretive discussion is that of C. H. Herford in his *Sketch of the History of the English Drama in its Social Aspects*. Comprehensive reviews of the whole matter are to be found in Chambers, Vols. I, VIII and IX and in the Cambridge History, Vol. VI. (An excellent summary by J. Dover Wilson.)

[2] Some of the exemplars of the drama I have discussed in Chapters I and II.

write histories that are knowon, as the life of Pompie, the martial affaires of Caesar, and other worthies, they give them a newe face and turne them out like counterfeites to showe themselves on the stage. . . . . "[3]

Such "sights and fond pastimes" their authors continued to offer as moral drama, either bodging up some morality material with them or bringing on a prologue to cast out fear from the hearts of the queasy auditors. The morality tradition was still so strong and the sophistical apologies so convincing that few of the zealots of the '70's advocate abolition. They inveigh against the abuses of the playhouses but they will sometimes admit the usefulness of the plays. Even Gosson, who later became unqualifiedly opposed to the stage, as a result of the sarcastic answers to his first pamphlets, has a good word to say in the *School of Abuse* for certain plays (including his own!):

"The twoo prose bookes plaied at the Belsavage, where you shall finde never a woorde without wit, never a line without pith, never a letter placed in vaine. The Jew and Ptolome, showne at the Bull, the one representing the greediness of wordly chusers and bloody mindes of Usurers: The other very lively discribyng howe seditious estates with their owne devises, false friends, with their owne swoordes and rebellious commons in their owne snares are overthrowne, neither with Amorous gesture wounding the eye, nor with slovenly talke hurting the eres of the chast hearers. The Black Smiths daughter, and Catilines Conspiracies usually brought into the theater, the first containing the trechery of Turkes, the honourable bountye of a noble minde and the shining of vertue in distress, the last, because it is knowen too be a Pig of myne owne Sowe, I will speake the lesse of it; onely giving you to understand that the whole marke which I shot at in the woorke was too showe the rewarde of traytors in Catilin and the necessary government of learned men, in the person of Cicero, which forsees every danger that is likely to happen and forstalles it continually ere it take effect. Therefore I give these playes the commedation Maximius Tyrius gave too Homers works . . . ."[4]

The author of the *Third Blast of Retrait from Plaies and Theaters* whose description of the secularized drama is quoted above proffers hair-raising accounts of the effect of the actors' wanton gestures and filthy speech and their bawdy stories of vanquished chastity on good

[3] Reprinted in the *English Drama and the Stage*, ed. W. C. Hazlitt. This passage is found on page 145. The date on the title page is 1580. The author is not known but the circumstantial evidence points to Munday.

[4] Arber reprint, p. 40. Miss Gildersleeve speaks of "violently denunciatory pamphlets such as Northbrooke's *Treatise* in 1572, Gosson's *Schoole of Abuse*, in 1579." This is scarcely accurate. Even Northbrooke who is pretty severe allows academic plays under certain conditions.

wives but he does not demand a general proscription of the theaters.[5] Let the magistrates prevent Sunday playing and persuade the noblemen to keep their vagabond players at home.

These instances of a concessive attitude on the part of some of the leading defamers of the stage are not given in an attempt to minimize the significance of such bitter denunciations as those of John Stockwood who, on two occasions at least, August 24, 1578 and again the following May, assailed the drama from the pulpit at Paul's Cross. From the beginning there existed a group of irreconcilables who called for abolition or nothing and their prestige increased. But we must not lose sight of the fact, as it is easy to do with so much material available which dwells on the horrible vices committed in the theaters themselves, that some compromise might have been effected if events immediately following these preliminary attacks had not made this forever impossible.

From 1580-1584 the City authorities campaigned with particular vigor against the unwelcome theatrical companies in their midst. During each of these years they made some effort to put down the plays altogether or regulate them strictly. In 1580 there was trouble over riots at the Theater, the investigation of which the Council eventually took over. In 1581 it had to importune the City to allow the plays up again after the plague. This same year the Master of the Revels received a patent giving him wide authority over dramatic affairs; a rather vague grant of power but of great importance in the history of that office which eventually became an arbiter in the dramatic world. In the spring of 1582 the Mayor ordered that all "enterludes in publique places and the resort to the same shall wholy be prohibited as ungodly." The excuse, as usual, was the plague. The Council, however, vetoed the ordinance and performances continued both within and outside the City. The disastrous collapse of a scaffold at Paris Garden, interpreted as a wrathful judgment, in January of the next year, gave the Mayor another cause for ejecting the players. For a time performances ceased. The Queen was evidently exasperated at

---

[5] I cannot forbear a quotation. "Lovers finding women pitying ill-fortuned stage lovers use this as a lever to raise their prospects. Credite me, there can be found no stronger engine to batter the honestie as wel of wedded wives, as the hearing of common plaies. There wanton fables and pastorical songes of loves which they use in their comical discourses (al which are taken out of the secret armorie of Venus & practising bawderie) turne al chastitie upside downe. . . . ." (p. 143.)

this constant interference with the pleasure of her people—and her own as well, for the city actors frequently appeared at Court. In March the Queen's Company was organized by a selection of twelve of the best performers to be obtained. Henceforth one company, at least, would be certain of ample protection from the constant annoyance of the Mayor's ordinances. The next year the Puritans seem to have won a great victory. Their representatives sent before the Court received permission to suppress the playhouses in and about London. The order was never fully executed although playing ceased as usual for the period of the summer. The actors presented an elaborate petition to the Council the next fall which the City authorities answered at length, replying point by point to their arguments. The players proposed certain rules by which they were willing to be bound—regulations regarding the days and times of playing. The authorities proposed to the Council another set, more severe, of course. What final action was taken we do not know for the darkness of history falls at this important moment. At any rate the players continued to act and the City officials, apparently discouraged after five years of unrelenting and unrewarded effort gave up the fight for the time being.[6]

With the exception of a few minor prohibitions the next six years were free from aggressive attack on the part of the Mayor. During these years the new drama rose and superseded the old. It is significant that this brilliant burst of dramatic activity follows immediately on the removal of restrictions which had hampered the players previously. The theater had won but at a price which the English drama in later centuries would have to pay.

The conciliatory tone, audible occasionally in the vociferous treatises against the stage written in the '70's, is no longer heard. Stubbes, charging at all kinds of vice in 1583, theater-going among others, permits no concessions with the devil. In the first extant edition of his famous *Anatomie of Abuses* (A Preface to the Reader) he had spoken reasonably of plays and interludes:[7]

"That whereas in the processe of this my booke, I have intreated of certen exercyses usually practised amongst us, as namely of Playes and Enterludes. . . . . I would not have thee so to take mee, as though my speaches tended to the

6 This brief review draws heavily on Miss Gildersleeve's work, pp. 160-175.

7 "Printed at London by Richard Jones, Maij, 1583." The second edition which lacks the significant preface came out in August of the same year. Reprint in *New Shakespeare Society*, Series VI, no. 4.

overthrowe and utter disliking of all kynd of exercyses in generall: that is nothing my simple meaning. But the particulare Abuses which are crept into every one of these severall exercyses is the onely thing which I thinke worthie of reprehension. . . . ."[8]

The ancients permitted plays as "conducible to example of life and reformation of manners . . . . so that when honest and chast playes, tragedies and enterludes are used to these ends, for the Godly recreation of the mind, for the good example of life, for the avoyding of that which is evill, and learning of that which is good, than are they very tollerable exercyses. . . . ."[9] This passage is excised from the subsequent editions, a fact plainly indicating a change of heart for the attacks on plays and players in the body of the work is as virulent as any ascetic could desire. Something—could it have been the Paris Garden disaster or the exasperating interference of the Court and the Council in the City's business?—made Stubbes pipe a different tune after May 1583. Bishop Babington writing in the same year finds no excuses whatever for "these prophane and wanton stage playes or interludes."[10] Later attacks in the same decade evince the same uncompromising attitude.

Whatever bitter feeling the failure, 1580-1584, of the City authorities in regulating the players may have caused among the Puritans was certain to be augmented by the outcome of the Martin-Marprelate controversy of 1589. There for the first time the dramatists, who during all this period, as we have seen, took particular pains to conciliate the Puritans by didactic apologies and a strict adherence to conventional morality, allow themselves to be identified with the anti-Puritan party. It is possible to regard this significant event as the most important battle in the long warfare which ended with the Parliamentary act of 1642 closing the theaters. Late in 1588 attempt was made to kill Martin by dramatic satire, or better, abuse.[11] *Martin*

[8] p. X.

[9] Reprint in *New Shakespeare Society*, Series VI, pp. x-xi.

[10] Extracts from his *Exposition of the Ten Commandments* given by Furnivall in the appendix to his edition of Stubbes' *Anatomy*, p. 83.

[11] Gosson, *Plays Confuted* (1581), describes the *Play of Plays*, a contemporary morality directed against the zealots who deny the usefulness of honest recreation. *Life* is the hero; the forces contending for him are *Delight* and *Zeal*. The tone of this piece was evidently not acrimonious and shows the difference in the relations between the Puritans and the players in 1582 and 1589.

Junior's Epilog refers to performances ridiculing the Puritans.[12]   *A Pappe with a Hatchet* (?Lyly's) describes an appearance of Martin on the public stage with "a cocks combe, an apes face, a wolfs bellie, cats claws, etc." Nashe's *Returne of Pasquill* alludes to a scene in which Vetus Comoedia "brought foorth Divinitie wyth a scratcht face, hold- ing of her hart as if she were sicke, because Martin would have foxed [forced?] her, but myssing of his purpose, he left the print of his nayles uppon her cheekes, and poysoned her with a vomit which he ministred unto her, to make her cast uppe her dignities and promo- tions."[13]   The Protestant pamphlet, *Martin's Month's Mind,* says Martin appeared "attired like an ape on ye stage and was then shipt. . . . . He took verie grievouslie to be made a Maygame upon the stage. . . . ." This retaliation by the players to various attacks of the previous twenty years the Council had finally to deal with. A committee of censor- ship was appointed on which the City, the Bishop of London, and the Court were to be represented. The Court's deputy was the Master of the Revels whose appointment really marks "the end of municipal licensing and the rise of the Master . . . . to censoring power."[14]

The Martin-Marprelate controversy, politically, was a kind of test case, a premonition of the struggle which would begin in earnest and in the open when James came to the throne. When the dramatists chose to ally themselves with the High Church party (members of which were their patrons) their cause with the Puritan body of middle- class England was forever lost. *Martin Junior's Epilogue* says: "Fear none of these beasts, these pursuivants, these Mar-Martins, these stage-players, these prelates, these popes, these devils, and all they can do. . . . ."[15]   And later in the same pamphlet the indentification is again adverted to: "They (the players) in the action of dealing against Master Martin have gotten them many thousand eye-witnesses of their witless and pitiful conceits. And indeed they are marvellous fit upholders of Lambeth Palace, and the crown of Canterbury."[16]

Ridicule of the Puritans, in later Elizabethan drama a sure-fire

[12] A brief sketch of Martin's conflict with the Puritans may be found in William Pierce's *An Historical Introduction to the Marprelate Tracts,* London, 1908, pp. 221-223.

[13] Grosart edition, vol. I, p. 123.

[14] Gildersleeve, p. 177.

[15] *Marprelate Tracts,* ed. William Pierce, London, 1911, p. 328.

[16] *Ibid.,* p. 330. *The Reproofe of Martin Junior by his Elder Brother* adds another reference of this kind: "And the men of sin themselves, I mean the Canterbury Chaplains and the rest of his anti-Christian beasts, who bear

hit, now begins for there is no longer any reason or necessity for the dramatists to conceal their natural antipathy for the "godly." Neal says of the political and ecclesiastical struggle: "While there was any hopes of compromising matters between the Church and the Puritans the controversy was carried on with some decency; but when all hopes of accommodation were at an end, the contending parties loaded each other with nothing but reproaches."[17] This situation finds an exact parallel in the subsidiary contention between the Puritans and the stage. Mr. Thompson has collected an impressive number of plots, scenes, passages, and allusions from late Elizabethan and seventeenth century drama in which the playwrights, with varying degrees of warmth, indulge in satire of the precisians. Although the later drama contains by far the most of it, 1590 is the point at which the attack begins. Instances from *Dr. Faustus* have been cited (Chapter III). *A Knack to Know a Knave* (printed 1594) contains in the person of the Priest what is perhaps the earliest of many caricatures of Puritan preachers of the type of Jonson's Zeal-of-the-Land Busy. Although living at the court of the Saxon king Edgar, this Priest is a shrewd, avaricious, hypocritical precisian, as he frankly proclaims:

> And I among my brethren and my friends
> Doe still instruct them with my doctrine,
> And yea and nay goes through the world with us,
> Fie, not an oath we sweare for twentie poond,
> Brethren (say we) take heed by Adams fal,
> For by his sinnes we are condemned all.
> Thus preach we still unto our brethren,
> Though in our heart we never meane the thing:
> Thus doe we blind the world with holiness,
> And so by that are tearmed pure Precisians.

Chapman's *An Humourous Day's Mirth* (?1597) adds the first picture of the vain Puritan wife, technically chaste but exceedingly self-rightcous over the repulse she has administered her lover. It is through no fault of hers that she has remained faithful to her husband.

> Surely the world is full of vanity;
> A woman must take heed she do not hear
> A lewd man speak; for every woman cannot,
> When she is tempted, when the wicked fiend

his adominable mark, were content in a manner to turn his purpose from a serious matter to a point of jesting; wherewith they would have only rhymes and stage players (that is plain rogues . . . .) to deal." p. 352.

[17] *History of the Puritans*, 1755, vol. I, p. 395.

> Gets her into his snares, escape like me;
> For grace's measure is not so filled up,
> Nor so pressed down, in every one as me;
> But yet I promise you a little more:
> Well, I'll go seek my head, who shall take me in
> The gates of his kind arms, untouched of any.[18]

After 1600 a reference to the Puritan manner of dress or speech, to the supposed habit the sect displayed of showing the whites of their eyes in glancing toward heaven, any allusion to a nasal speech, to the refusal to take an oath, was as certain of a laugh as the old gags about a pair of gilded horns.

At first sight the Elizabethan drama may seem to have gained much and lost nothing by the alienation of men of the stamp of Gosson and Stubbes. And indeed for thirty years the gain was great. When forced to defend their art the contemporaries of Shakespeare reverted to the old moral arguments used by Lodge and Nashe but they really wrote, that is to say the greatest of them did, with a desire, not to reform but to interpret the life they saw about them. The immediate effect of the withdrawal of the irreconcilable Puritans was an almost instant loss of a pronounced didactic tone in the drama. But by 1625 the theater had become pretty much the exclusive property of the higher classes of society by the gradual exodus of the citizens' and their wives to the Puritan camp. The companies had long since been placed under the patronage of the royal family and a Court functionary, the Master of the Revels, was now the arbiter in questions of dramatic propriety. The great plays of Jonson were now a part of stage history. The old-fashioned dramatists whose work sounded the praise of a new England had for the most part ceased to write. A group of younger men for whom the Court rather than the City was the center of existence had arrived to fill their places. As a result the ensuing drama became narrow in scope and imaginatively sterile—reflecting the interests of only one social class. Its fall was inevitable upon the political decline of that class.

The English middle classes have never been induced to come back to the theater which they began to leave in 1580. The English theater remains to-day, in spite of a recent notable Renaissance, the function of a single class. Quite otherwise is the condition in France and Germany where it is now, and always has been, as necessary to the common life as sport or any other "lawful exercise."

[18] Scene 14, ll. 125-134.

V

THE LATER PLAYWRIGHTS AND DIDACTICISM

With the disappearance in the years after 1590 of the need for conciliating the radically Puritan spectators and the change in the status of the playwright effected through the efforts of the professional dramatists, patent didacticism retires from the Elizabethan stage. But it is by no means entirely lacking, in a mild form at least, in several of the successors to Marlowe, Peele, and Greene. The new group of writers, most of them at one time or another bound to Henslowe, from which individuals begin to emerge from the anonymity of collaboration toward the end of the century, contains four men who profess or demonstrate at times a moral purpose in their writing: Dekker, Heywood, Jonson, and Chapman. The first two belong in the native tradition both as regards their dramatic practise and their attitude toward the question of the stage and morality. Jonson and Chapman, professed classicists, derived not only their opinions of the laws of dramatic structure but their apology for the art from the authors whom they revered.

Dekker nowhere expressly defends the stage or declares his intention to reform his fellow men. As a matter of fact in the one place where he adverts to the purpose of his writing he would seem to uphold an extreme aesthetic theory of his art. The address, prefixed to the *Shoemakers' Holiday,* to "All good fellows, professors of the gentle craft, of what degree soever," concludes with the words:

Take all in good worth that is well intended, for nothing is purposed but mirth; mirth lengtheneth long life, which with all other blessings, I heartily wish you. Farewell![1]

But he finds it convenient in other plays to give the story a moral twist. In developing the folk tales of Fortunatus and Friar Rush he does not miss an occasion to add the didactic strain. His greatest drama, *The Honest Whore,* is not free from it though the penitent words of Bellafront, sincere and deep-sprung as they are, seem appropriate enough in their place:

Oh, when the work of lust had earned my bread.
To taste it how I trembled, lest each bit,

[1] Mermaid Edition, p. 4.

Ere it went down, should choke me chewing it!
My bed seemed like a cabin hung in hell.
The bawd, hell's porter, and the liquorish wine
The pander fetched, was like an easy fine,
For which, me thought, I leased away my soul.
And oftentimes, even in my quaffing bowl,
Thus said I to myself, I am a whore,
And have drunk down thus much confusion more.[2]

Dekker's extant work shows him to have been a humanitarian before the term was known and apparently deeply religious as well, if the fine prayers contained in the *Foure Birdes of Noahs Arke* are indicative. His religion seems to have had little charity in it for the church of Rome, however, if the evidence of the violently anti-Catholic play, *The Whore of Babylon,* and the tract named *The Double P.P.* may be trusted for autobiographic inference. In the *Dead Term* (1608) he exposes the sins of London and Westminster. *A Rod for Runawayes* bids the fugitives from the plague consider how God has visited his judgment on the City. Verses prefacing his *Lanthorn and Candlelight,* a further exposé, in Greene's manner, of low life in London, praise him as a flagellator of abuses, one who takes "sinnes hight as men doe sterres aloofe." As a pamphleteer at least, he had an established reputation for morality and plaindealing.

A Fortunatus play, evidently in two parts, was revived by the Admiral's Men, February, 1596. In November, 1599 Dekker received £6 from Henslowe for the "hole history of Fortunatus." For a subsequent court production he added the allegorical machinery of the contest between Virtue and Vice. Either Dekker or the original author has given the play a religious cast which the story does not possess. There Fortune is pictured simply as the goddess Fortuna who dispenses gifts to men. She in no way suggests that there is a dire fatality implied in Fortunatus' wish to have wealth instead of wisdom. The incident has been given a Faustian significance which is further emphasized at the death of the hero. Similarly the first son, Andelosia, is made to appear a conscious sinner. His last words declare his contrition:

O conscience, hold thy sting, cease to afflict me.
Be quick, tormentors, I desire to die;
No death is equal to my misery,
Cyprus, vain world and vanity, farewell.
Who builds his Heaven on earth, is sure of hell.[3]

[2] Part II, Mermaid Edition, p. 255.
[3] Mermaid edition, p. 379.

The German tale represents him as well beloved, so general a favorite in fact that after his death he is buried in the cathedral church with great honour.[4]

The more important addition for which Dekker alone is surely responsible is, of course, the morality-masque which ends the play. Vice and Virtue war over Andelosia much as the Good and Bad Angels struggle for the soul of Faustus. As Herford has suggested, the necessity for the final triumph of Virtue forced the author into a difficult situation. He had already represented Fortune as on the side of morality in making her rebuke Fortunatus' choice. And so Virtue's evident dislike of her must be put down as a kind of professional jealousy. But the symmetry of the masque had to be maintained and the Queen complimented and Dekker, as usual, was little troubled by the more exquisite torments of an artistic conscience.

Though modern critics are not inclined to agree with him, the prologue to Dekker's *If this be not a Good Play, the Devil is in It*, felt he was presenting a play of superlative merit. He slights the contemporary dramatists for their lack of high moral tone:

> But 'tis with Poets now, as 'tis with Nations,
> Thil-savourdst Vices, are the bravest Fashions.
> A Play whose Rudenes, Indians would abhorre,
> Ift fill a house with Fishwives, Rare, They all Roare.
> It is not Praise is sought for (Now) but Pence,
> Tho dropd from Greasie-apron Audience.[5]

A more inapposite apology was never offered in an Elizabethan theater be a reputable playwright, for the play is a jumbled and incoherent piece of work. The story tells of the frustrated efforts of three subdevils to corrupt the city of Naples. They leave Pluto's realm to attack severally the Court, the City, and the best monastery in the region, reputed for the virtue and the charity of its monks. Their machinations temporarily succeed but the subverted King eventually sees the right and undertakes to reform the mischief which has been done. Although the spectacular scenes in Hell and such exhibitions as the Glittering Head and Ruffman's fire-works were intended to awe and delight the denizens of the pit while the satire on the Puritans

---

[4] The alterations which Dekker made are fully described by C. H. Herford, *The Literary Relations of England and Germany in the Sixteenth Century*, Cambridge, 1886, pp. 210-218. The German story is available in K. Simrock's *Die deut. Volksbücher*, 3er Band.

[5] *Dramatic Works of Thomas Dekker*, ed. by Pearson, Vol. III, p. 263.

and the punishments inflicted on Fawkes and Ravillac were calculated
to feed their religious prejudices, there is an undoubted undercurrent
of seriousness in the play. It is no frank satire on devil-plays like
Jonson's *The Devil is an Ass*. The demons are frustrated, not because
they are stupid and incompetent, but because good men have power
over them.

In the *Honest Whore* Dekker the moralist as well as humanitarian
is revealed. Specific discussion of the play has been reserved for a
later chapter. It is enough to say here that none of his contemporaries
who have harsh words to say of ladies of Bellafront's profession, speak
with so much vehemence. In Part I (II, 1) the speeches which Hippolito directs at Bellafront and which work her salvation leave nothing
to be added. Yet Dekker manages to reverse the situation in the
second part when Bellafront answers her saviour's solicitations with a
harrowing description of the harlot's life (IV, 1). Though both
passages are obviously extended for their effect, Dekker has accomplished the rare feat of absorbing didactic material into the body of
his play, motivating its use and giving it the stamp of the characters
who are entrusted with it.[6]

With Thomas Heywood we have a unique opportunity for knowing
what relationship he felt existed between the stage and life since he
left his dramatic creed for future critics to examine. The *Apology
for Actors* differs in several particulars from similar defenses of the
stage which preceded it. Other playwrights, notably Nashe and Lodge,
had replied to the enemies of their profession but *Pierce Penniless* and
the *Defense of Poetry, Musick and Stage-Plays* are in part only devoted
to the question of the propriety of dramatic performances. Nashe
pauses in the midst of a satiric supplication to the Devil for aid in
his poverty to have a bout with those enemies of poetry who "tearme
our best writers but babbling ballet-makers." His defense has this
in common with Heywood's elaborate treatise that both men rely on

---

[6] Dekker's achievement in the *Honest Whore* becomes more apparent when
his play, particularly the second part, is compared with Sharpham's *The Fleire*,
contemporary with it and resembling it in certain details of plot. The disguised
Fleire, like Orlando, Bellafront's father, enters the service of his two daughters
who are courtesans. But the author has attempted to make a tragi-comedy out
of his materials and, to provide comedy, requires Fleire to rail at the vice of
whoredom while countenancing the waywardness of his daughters. He is a
malcontent figure of the Marstonian variety but the situation in which Sharpham
places him is scarcely edifying.

arguments drawn from the state of the contemporary English theater as well as the usual citations from pagan writers who praised the stage. Lodge's pamphlet attempted to fend off Gosson's attack on music, poetry and the innocent pastimes of dicing and tumbling. As in the case of Nashe his commendation of dramatic art is incidental to his main theme. He confines his argument, moreover, almost entirely to the classical authorities. Heywood essays a treatise which shall canvass the subject completely and in an unimpassioned manner. He is "profest adversary to none" but wishes only reconcilement. The whole defense is free from vituperative recrimination and maintains a serenity of tone entirely possible at a time when the acting profession was honoured and the position of the theater secure under a sovereign who had given it his direct patronage. Although the first two portions of the essay rest on the usual pleas of the antiquity and ancient dignity of the profession, Heywood is most easy and persuasive when he speaks of the actual benefits which the theater he had helped to make great had conferred on English life. Nashe was the first to praise the native dramatists; Heywood follows his lead. There is no city in Christendom which offers more variety of entertainment. The stage has so far refined the English tongue that men are now ashamed of the speech that sixty years ago the most discriminating were "proud to pronounce." The ignorant have been made more apprehensive so that men may now discourse of any notable thing "from the landing of Brute until this day." But the final argument is inevitably the much-used moral argument. Tragedies terrify men and restrain their murderous proclivities. The stories of Pompey, Alexander, Mydas, Nero, Sardanapalus, and Ninus hold them from the vices which the lives of these great men exemplified. The *Apology* concludes with two examples of miraculous reformations wrought by the witnessing of plays; one occurring at Linn in Norfolk when the Earl of Sussex' players acted the *Old History of Feyr Francis* so vividly that a murderess in the audience cried out her sin, the other in Amsterdam where the English comedians moved another criminal to confession.[7]

If we did not possess this valuable apology we should still be able to surmize that Heywood believed his art justified by its value as a

---

[7] The first of these incidents is told by Master James in *A Warning for Fair Women* (1076-1087). Apparently it was a stock illustration with defenders of the stage.

warning and an example to men. He seldom fails to moralize his
dramatic situations, as a few instances will show. In part one of
If You Know Not Me, You Know Nobody, the Lord Mayor presents
Queen Elizabeth with a Bible. She pauses to sermonize:

> Who lookes for joy, let him this booke adore;
> This is true food for rich men and for poore.
> Who drinkes of this is certaine ne'er to perish:
> This will the soule with heavenly vertue cherish. [8]

In the second part Dean Nowell, while showing the portraits of London's virtuous Lord Mayors to Gresham, Sir Thomas Ramsie and their
attendants, rises to the occasion and delivers the following lecture:

> If you will follow the religious path
> That these have beat before you, you shall win Heaven. . . . .
> O is't not better that young couples say,
> You rais'd us up, then, you were our decay?
> And mothers tongues teach their first borne to sing
> Of your good deeds, then by your bad to wring? [9]

Haring in the *Wise Woman of Hogsdon* exhorts his companions against
the abuse of dicing:

> Let's not like debosht fellowes, play our Clothes
> Belts, Rapiers, nor our needfull ornaments:
> 'Tis childish, not becoming Gentlemen.
> Play was at first ordayn'd to passe the time;
> And sir, you but abuse the use of Play,
> To employ it otherwise. [10]

The Captain in *Royal King and Loyal Subject* inveighs against whores
much in the style of Dekker's Hippolito:

> You are not women, you are devils both,
> And that your Damme; my body save in warres,
> Is yet unskarr'd, nor shall it be with you.
> Say the least leacher that unbrac't you here,
> And folded in his armes your rottennesse,
> Had beene all these, would not all that filth
> Vomite on me? or who would buy diseases,
> And make his body for a Spittle fit,
> That may walke sound? I came to school you whoore,
> Not to corrupt you. . . . . [11]

The archaistic *Four Prentices of London* teaches an excellent morality.
The heroine is ready to sacrifice her life unless her protectors compound

[8] Pearson edition, Vol. I, p. 246.
[9] *Ibid.,* p. 278.
[10] *Ibid.,* Vol. V, p. 282.
[11] Edition of Kate M. Tibbals, Univ. of Penn. Series, Vol. XII, p. 96.

the quarrel which has brought them near a "general overthrow." Charles, who has become the captain of a band of outlaws, with all the nobility of Schiller's robber Moor, commands his men to beware of doing evil:

> Hee that committs a rape, shall sure be hang'd;
> Hee that commits a murder, shall be murdered
> With that same weapon that did act the deed.
> Hee that robbes pilgrims, or poore Travellours
> That for devotions sake do passe these Mountaines,
> Hee shall be naked tyed to armes of Trees,
> And in the dayes heate stung with Waspes and Bees.[12]

When Heywood surveyed the drama of the 1630's he felt that his day had passed. He found the stage-subjects now puling lovers, crafty bawds and cheats. No longer were the "valours of such men whose very names might dignify the pen" proclaimed in the theater. Typical of the man but not of the age into which he had lived is his apology for the title of his late play, *A Mayden-head Well Lost* (1634):

> Courteous Reader (of what sexe soever) let not the Title of this Play anyway deterro thee from the perusall thereof: For there is nothing herein contained, which doth deviate either from Modesty or good Manners. For though the argument be drawne from a Maydenhead lost, yet to be well lost cleares it from all aspersion.

Since Beaumont's *Knight of the Burning Pestle* is an obvious burlesque of the kind of play which Heywood purveyed to his burgher audience there may be a covert allusion to his constant though sincere playing up to the moral prejudices of his public, in the prologue's introduction to Ralph's play:

> Fly far from hence
> All private taxes, immodest phrases,
> What ere may but shew like vicious!
> For wicked mirth never true pleasure brings,
> But honest minds are pleas'd with honest things.

At any rate, whether they are intended as satire or not, these lines do fairly well characterize the moral tone of Heywood's drama.

Ben Jonson's view of the stage as an arbiter of morals, though in some respects in agreement with Heywood's, was arrived at by a far different process. The contrast between the two men is striking; Heywood, the true actor, with an ear to the wishes of his audience, vulgarized his themes and followed, except in the case of *A Woman Killed With Kindness*, the dramatic fashions established by others.

[12] Pearson edition, Vol. II, p. 182.

His morality is not so much a matter of logical conviction as feeling and a kind of unconscious response to the taste of his public. Jonson defied the *vulgus* when they refused to accept his austere and censorious productions and his plea was always that the crowd had no understanding of the high seriousness of his art. He never grew weary of telling the requirements of a "true poem," tragic or comic. In the character of Asper (*Every Man Out of His Humour*) he speaks as he might have done among his friends in the Apollo Room of the Devil Tavern when crabs were hissing in the fire:

> Good men, and virtuous spirits, that loathe their vices,
> Will cherish my free labours, love my lines,
> And with the fervor of their shining grace
> Make my brain fruitful, to bring forth more objects,
> Worthy of their serious and intentive eyes.
>   . . . . my strict hand
> Was made to seize on vice, and with a gripe
> Squeeze out the humour of such spongy souls,
> As lick up every idle vanity.[13]

For nearly forty years he anatomized the vices, major and minor, of his city, striking at sham, avarice, superstition, extortion and maintaining against the old-fashioned dramatists with their want of art and the new court dramatists with their want of seriousness the responsibility and the dignity of his profession.

It was characteristic of the man that he should turn to the universities for justification upon the failure of his *Sejanus* wherein he had taught insolent men how dangerous pride is and the odious wisdom of blasphemy. In dedicating *Volpone* to them he sets forth his *credo*. He there places himself with Milton, Coleridge, and Shelley in declaring "the impossibility of any man's being the good poet, without first being a good man." None of the Renaissance critics valued higher the calling of the poet than Jonson when he said he is "able to inform young men in all good disciplines, inflame grown men to all great virtues, keep old men in their best and supreme state, or, as they decline to childhood, recover them to their first strength; that comes forth the interpreter and arbiter of nature, a teacher of things divine no less than human, a master of manners, and can alone or with a few, effect the business of mankind."[14] That the dramatic writers

---

[13] Cunningham edition, Vol. I, p. 67.

[14] Cunningham edition, Vol. I, pp. 333-335. Minturno, *De Poeta,* Venice, 1559, pp. 8-9, furnishes the original for the phraseology of this particular passage.

of the age have fallen sadly from this high ideal he is ready to admit but for himself, "I can, and from a most clear conscience, affirm that I have ever trembled to think toward the least profaneness; have loathed the use of such foul and unwashed bawdry, as is now made the food of the scene. . . . ." His hands are clean though on the present stage only the "filth of the time is uttered, and with such impropriety of phrase, such plentitude of solecisms . . . . with brothelry able to violate the ear of a pagan, and blasphemy to turn the blood of a Christian to water. . . . ." This particular play, *Volpone,* has a double object: to present a story innocently and properly which shall "inform men in the best reason of living" and put a "snaffle in their mouths that cry out, we never punish vice in our interludes."

Echoes of this preface resound in various of Jonson's works. In the *Discoveries* he declares the parts of comedy and tragedy are the same and the end is partly the same for they both teach and delight.[15] *Love's Triumph Through Callipolis* is foreworded with a note which explains that all "representations, especially those of this nature in court, public spectacles, either have been, or ought to be, the mirrors of a man's life, whose ends, for the excellence of their exhibitors— ought always to carry a mixture of profit with them no less than delight."[16] The Prologue to the *Staple of News* describes the poet as one "that can instruct the youth and keep your acme in the state of truth." The Epilogue steps forward to say:

> Thus have you seen the maker's double scope
> To profit and delight. . . . .

Although Jonson is a thorough-going neo-classicist as regards the function of the dramatist, his theory is not allowed to confound his practise any more than it is in the matter of the observance of the "rules." Jonson's didacticism, in spite of its kinship with that of the first group of Senecans in England, is no impediment to his interpretation of life and manners. He is usually contented to be a recorder. The sermons are confined for the most part to the indignant prefaces which abuse the public for failing to interpret correctly what he has painstakingly furnished for their instruction as well as their delight. There is much to be learned of his attitude in an aside, *To the Reader,* prefixed to the *Alchemist:*

. . . . for thou wert never more fair in the way to be cozened, than in this age, in Poetry, especially in Plays: wherein now the concupiscence of dances

[15] "The parts of a comedy and tragedy," Cunningham ed., Vol. III, p. 422.

[16] Cunningham edition, Vol. III, p. 200.

and antics so reigneth, as to run away from nature, and be afraid of her, is the only point of art that tickles the spectators.[17]

Jonson was never afraid of nature and he never tried to run away from her.   In these few lines he takes his place with the exponents of the higher morality who believes no harm can come to men who look at the whole of life with steady eyes.   This is a point of view very different from that of earlier neo-classical moralists who modified the stories which they used in the interests of a conventional morality.

George Chapman sets forth a view of the stage in a passage in *The Revenge of Bussy D'Ambois* which, appearing gratuitously as it does, may well be taken as his authentic opinion.   Clermont, who is Chapman's Senecal man, his perfect hero, turns from an invective against the popular theaters where men come to laugh and "feed fool-fat" to praise the stage as it should be:

> . . . . and stages too
> Have a respect due to them, if but only,
> For what the good Greek moralist says of them:
> "Is a man proud of greatness, or of riches?
> Give me an expert actor, I'll show all
> That can within his greatest glory fall.
> Is a man fray'd with poverty and lowness?
> Give me an actor, I'll show every eye
> What he laments so, and so much doth fly,
> The best and worst of both."   If but for this then,
> To make the proudest outside, that most swells
> With things without him and above his worth,
> See how small cause he has to be blown up,
> And the poor man to be griev'd with poorness,
> Both being so easily borne by expert actors,
> The stage and actors are not so contemptful
> As every innovating Puritan,
> And ignorant sweater-out of zealous envy,
> Would have the world imagine.[18]

The dedication of this same play to Sir Thomas Howard contains the usual moral justification for dramatic writing:

Poor envious souls they are that cavil at truth's want in these natural fictions; material instruction, elegant and sententious excitation to virtue, and deflection from her contrary, being the soul, limbs and limits of an authentical tragedy. . . . .[19]

Of all the Elizabethan dramatists Chapman is the most philosophic.

[17] *Ibid.*, Vol. II, p. 3
[18] I, 1, 333-351.
[19] Parrott edition, p. 77.

This becomes evident not so much from the fact that his plays are interlined with sententious passages on the usual problems of life, death, fate, and necessity, as in the quality of thought which these passages contain. Chapman's age accepted with avidity ideas which came to it from the continent. Chapman is inclined to question mental habits old or new. Consider as an instance his attitude toward the conception of *virtu*. Raleigh and Drake, Leicester and Essex exemplified it. The dramatists, beginning with Marlowe, poetized it. It becomes as much a part of the morality of the Elizabethan drama as the older theological dogmas had been of the moral interludes. But Chapman makes his Clermont say:

> Let all fall that would rise unlawfully:
> Make not your forward spirit in virtues right,
> A property for vice, by thrusting on
> Further than all your powers can fetch you off. . . . .
> Let virtue some good from your graces gather:
> Avarice of all is ever nothing's father.[20]

Or consider his treatment of women. Some of his comedies show a decided cynicism in contrast with the usual attitude of his contemporaries, none of whom, with the exception of Marston, went so far as he in exposing the frailty of the sex. He seems to have written *An Humourous Day's Mirth, May-Day,* and *A Widow's Tears* from definite conviction. In the two Bussy plays, as I shall try to demonstrate later, he departs even farther from the accepted and conventional point of view in an attempt to understand the character of Tamyra whom he has created with painstaking care.

Chapman repeats in at least three places the dangerous doctrine that a virtuous man is above the law. The best statement of this principle, which runs directly contrary to the spirit of the Jacobean régime, occurs in the *Gentleman Usher:*

> And what's a prince? Had all been virtuous men,
> There never had been prince upon the earth,
> And so no subject; all men had been princes; ·
> A virtuous man is subject to no prince,
> But to his soul and honour.[21]

And so, although it is right to say that Chapman belongs with the moralists among the Elizabethan dramatists, one must be careful to

---

[20] V. 1, 69-77.

[21] V, 4, 56-60. Also Cato's words, *Caesar and Pompey*, V, 2, 8-21, and *Bussy*, II, 1, 200-204.

observe that the morality he taught was often at variance with that
which was generally sanctioned by his contemporaries.   As in the
case of Jonson, though for a different reason, his didactic purpose
did not prevent his attempting to present poetic truth as he envisaged
it.

A diligent search in the minor drama of the later Elizabethan
period yields only a few instances of obtrusive didacticism.   Daborne
writing his *Christian Turned Turk* (printed 1612) made it plain that
he intended to "take a higher pitch" than others who had preceded
him in the use of his spectacular story.   Through the medium of the
Chorus he succeeds in impressing on his audiences the moral significance of the scene they are to witness.   While the Christian abjures,
in dumb show, his native faith, the Chorus laments his fall:

> (He) Forsweares his name! with what, we blush to tell,
> But 'tis no wonder, blackes the way to hell.
> Who though he seeme yet happy, his successe
> Shewes he exchang'd with it (but) wretchednesse.
> Give patience to our Scoene, which herto tends,
> To show the world, blacke deeds will have blacke ends.[22]

In a class with Daborne's play but even more extravagant in its exhibition of wickedness is Barnes' *Devil's Charter*.   The theme itself is
sufficiently moral, being the story of another devil-compact resembling
Faustus' but the grossness of some of the scenes, one may surmize,
required the aureole of sanctimoniousness which surrounds the play,
if it were to pass public censure.[23]

During the decade from 1600 to 1610 the breach between the
Puritans and the stage widened still farther.   The satire of the sect
which had been largely confined to single characters or injected comments on the peculiarities of the "godly" now broadened until it ab-
sorbed a large part of the action of such plays as *The Puritan* and *The
Family of Love*.   The private theaters flourished during this era and
the attitude of the court began to be the determining factor in the

[22] The play is reprinted in *Anglia*, Vol. XX.   This passage is on page 227.

[23] This later drama is not lacking in paragons of female virtue who are ready
to encourage others to follow their example.   Although the general problem of
didacticism in matters of sexual morality is considered in the second part of
this thesis, I may be permitted to mention here the well-named Modestia of the
pseudo-Shakespearean *Birth of Merlin*.   Her every entrance is a signal for a
preachment.   She refuses to have a husband and even succeeds in persuading her
sister to abandon hers at the door of the church.   Winifred in Rowley's *Shoe-
maker a Gentleman* for all her piety cannot hold a candle to her.

future of the stage. There is evidence to show that a portion of the Elizabethan audience had grown weary of didactic plays and dramatists whose intention it was to reform the age. Day in his exceedingly amusing induction to the *Isle of Gulls* allows his First Gentlemen, who is talking to the Prologue just come out on to the stage, to satirize the section of the public which still asked for moral plays:

First Gent. But what method observes hee [the author] in his play? ist any thing Criticall? Are Lawyers fees and Citizens wives laid open in it? I love to heare vice anatomized & abuse let blood in the maister vaine: is there any great mans life charactred int?

Prologue. None I protest, sir: only in the person of Dametas he expresses to the life the monstrous and deformed shape of vice, as well to beget a lothing of abuse as that his villaine may give the greater luster to the vertuous dispositions of true-borne gentilitie.

First Gent. All thats nothing to mee: and there be not Wormewood water and Copperas int Ile not like it, should Apollo write it and Rosius himself act it.[24]

At least one of the later contemporaries of Shakespeare openly renounced the didactic theory of the function of the drama and declared the giving of pleasure alone his aim as a dramatist. Jonson, referring no doubt to Marston's habit of satire, said to William Drummond that he "wrote his Father-in-lawes preachings and his Father-in-law his Commedies." Yet it is difficult to believe that Marston had any reformatory intention in his playwriting. It is doubtful if the true satirist, which Marston claimed to be, ever hopes to convince men of their folly and turn them to better ways. Certainly his dramatic commentators like Quadratus, Felice, Hercules, and the Malcontent, satirists who speak for their author, are too much disillusioned about the possibility of virtue's eventual triumph in the world to labor for it. There is much assaulting of vice, particularly sexual vice, in the plays and one of them, *The Dutch Courtesan*, is definitely planned to show the "difference betwixt the love of a courtesan and a wife." But Marston's attitude toward the art of the dramatist, in so far as it can be deduced from his prologues and forewords is not that of the reformer or conscious moralist. He affects a casualness toward his work amounting now and then to something like depreciation which stands, perhaps, in intentional contrast to Jonson's serious and conscientious manner. The Prologue to *Antonio and Mellida* offers a "worthless present of slight idleness." This same flippancy is repeated in the Induction to *What You Will* where the play is referred to as a "slight

[24] Bullen's *Day,* Vol. I, p. 5.

toy, lightly composed, too swiftly finished, ill-plotted, worse-written.
. . . ." Doricus seems to be hitting at Jonson covertly when he declares
music and poetry are approved by rules of common-sense and that
which is pleasing is most allowed:

> . . . . know, rules of art
> Were shaped to pleasure, not pleasure to your rules.

He is ready to appeal to the popular verdict; the favorable judgment
of three or four compels no acceptance by the rest of the world.

Marston's most moral play, *The Dutch Courtesan*, is prologued
with a passage which maintains this idea that the spectators' pleasure
is the ultimate justification of the dramatist's labours:

> . . . . the only end
> Of our now study is, not to offend.
> Yet think not but, like others rail we could
> (Best art presents not what it can but should)
> And if our pen in this seems over-slight,
> We strive not to instruct, but to delight. . . . .[25]

It might seem as if *Sophonisba, or the Wonder of Women*, were intended to display the virtues of the sex to which this astounding heroine
belongs.   But Marston appears to regard her conduct as anomalous,
something to be wondered at along with the deeds of the witch Erichtho
and the activities of the ghost of Asdrubal.   The Epilogus in asking
for applause justifies his request because the scenes have been exempt
from ribaldry and rage and taxings indiscreet.   He says no word of
the morality of the play.

The preface to the "Equal Reader" prefixed to the *Fawn* sets forth
in detail Marston's theory of comedy.   Jonson, it will be remembered,
declared the imitation of justice to be his aim.   Marston identifies the
purpose of comedy with that of satire, quoting from Juvenal:

> Quicquid agunt homines, votum, timor, ira, voluptas,
> Gaudia, discursus, nostri farrago libelli est.

The prologue flatly asserts:

> Your modest pleasure is our author's scope,
> The hurdle and the rack to them he leaves
> That have naught left to be accompted any. . . . .
> But if the nimble form of comedy,
> Mere spectacle of life and public manners,
> May gracefully arrive to your pleased ears,
> We boldly dare the utmost death of fears. . . . .[26]

[25] Bullen's edition, Vol. II, p. 5.
[26] Bullen's edition, Vol. II, p. 114.

It is perhaps a significant fact that Lyly and Marston who, almost alone, among the Elizabethans, propose to rest their claim to consideration by their audiences on the amount of pleasure they can give them should both have been connected with private playhouses. Both were men who delighted more in words than the ideas which they express. Both lacked the religious fervor or the critical faculty which makes men reformers. Although Marston reiterates that his work is free from the vices of bawdry and railing, his plays are full of both. His declaration that he wishes by them only to give pleasure is, however, justified by the quality of his art.

We have seen that two of Shakespeare's friends and rivals, Dekker and Heywood, belong to a degree with the older men in whose work traces of the didactic purpose linger. With Jonson and Chapman the moral purpose, though consciously set forth, seldom hampers the free play of their intellect and imagination. With Beaumont and Fletcher and Webster the didactic element passes from Elizabethan drama. These later men came into the profession when the English Renaissance had entered upon a new phase. The seventeenth century, their century, inaugurates the modern era in which man has rediscovered his own mind and has been less and less ready therefore to trust irrational standards imposed from without. The new paganism begins with Francis Bacon and his contemporaries and the drama reflects this changing attitude toward life. It would be easy to press this observation to an absurdity but it is obvious, nevertheless, that certain of the Jacobean dramatists attacked their problems as the most imaginative of scientists do, not to corroborate and teach but to record and interpret. Shakespeare stands preëminent in this instance. Webster, alone, approaches him because he, alone, among his fellows had in any such degree the two qualities which Shakespeare by implication requires of the dramatic poet, the ability to "hold as 'twere, the mirror up to nature, to show virtue her own feature, scorn her own image, and the very age and body of the time his form and pressure" and the imagination which can penetrate beyond the superficial to the "forms of things unknown."

PART TWO

I

THE POSITION OF WOMEN IN THE ELIZABETHAN DRAMA

The Law, the Church, and Tudor Women

It is not too much to say that for the first time in the history of western civilization the various problems that arise from the relations between the sexes received full and minute consideration in the drama written during the reigns of Elizabeth and James. Twice previously—in twelfth century France and fifteenth century Italy—woman had been accorded a prominent position in literature but the view of society which this chivalric and courtly poetry presents, seen in the one instance through the mist of *l'amour courtois* and in the other colored by Neo-Platonic tints, can scarcely be trusted as precise and realistic. That is one reason why Chaucer's marriage group stands in sharp relief against the conventional background of medieval love poetry. We recognize as individual and authentic the portrait of the Wife of Bath. Yet understanding of woman's nature and the problems which her mere existence in the world creates was not granted instantly to the Elizabethan dramatists. There lies a world of difference between the conception of the sinning heroine in *Gismond of Salerne,* made to order, as it were, in accord with a set convention, and the magnificently isolated figure of Vittoria in the *White Devil.* In the interval between, one finds experiment with many themes and situations, finds the romantic and codified treatment of them gradually abandoned for a more penetrative study based on the observation of human actions. A consideration of this growth in the understanding of woman's nature in Elizabethan drama, as revealed in the dramatization of moral problems in which her character is a factor, must constitute a large part of any study of its technical and philosophical development.[1]

[1] A brief survey of the available criticism may not be amiss.
1. Marie Gothein, "Die Frau im englischen Drama vor Shakespeare," *Jahrbuch* xl, pp. 1-50. Complete and detailed as far as it goes.

The starting point for such a consideration should be the evidence relating to woman's position in Tudor society furnished by the remaining contemporaneous literature and especially the legal and ecclesiastical provisions regulating her conduct. Yet we should not be too credulous in examining the mass of available evidence. The law rarely keeps pace with the times and the church demands the impossible of frail humanity. The Elizabethan novel is worse than useless as a picture of Elizabethan domestic life; the "domestic conduct book," written by pious churchmen and directed like the woman's magazine of the present toward a particular group in society, may only be trusted if read with circumspection. Better than the official documents are the illuminating flashes of truth from the scanty gossip of the time and the observations of foreigners visiting in England. Legally the women of Tudor England profited little by the Reformation. In other Protestant countries the views of Luther and Calvin on marriage had been erected into laws. Absolute divorce was permitted for adultery and desertion, and the old Popish distinction between a nullifying divorce, granted upon the discovery of impediments to the marriage and allowing remarriage, and the divorce of separation *a thoro et a mensa* given for a number of causes but not allowing remarriage, had been entirely done away with. In England the ecclesiastical courts, arranged in an ascending series of five degrees, still judged marriage difficulties as in earlier days. Officially there could be no absolute divorce except upon the discovery that the marriage had been illegally contracted, e.g., within the forbidden degrees of affinity.[2] Actually the *divortium a*

---

2. Ortgies Siefken, *Die Konstanze-Griseldistypus in der Eng. Lit. bis auf Shakespere*, Rathenow, 1903. The drama claims only a few pages and there is no attempt at interpretation.

3. Heinrich Diestel, *Die schuldlos verdächtigte Frau im elisabethanischen Drama*, Rostock, 1909. Supplements no. 1.

4. Willy Thomann, *Der eifersüchtige Ehemann im Drama der eliz. Zeit.*, Halle, 1908. Touches the present problem at only one point.

5. Chilton Powell, *English Domestic Relations, 1487-1653*, New York, 1917, Chapter vi, 2-"Domestic Drama." Not so penetrating as it should be considering the mass of collateral material accumulated.

6. A. H. Quinn, Edition of the *Faire Maide of Bristow*, Philadelphia, 1902, pp. 24-25. Gives a brief account of some of the Patient Wife plays.

C. H. Herford's essay *Shakespeare's Treatment of Love and Marriage*, in a volume of that title, should not be overlooked.

[2] There is a delightful parody of the divorce law in *Epicene*, Act V. The divorce *a thoro et a mensa* is ridiculed in *All Fools*, IV, when the Notary reads the bill.

thoro et a mensa came to be regarded as a license for the remarriage of the innocent party.[3] The institution of marriage itself remained much as it had been before Henry's marital difficulties got his people a new spiritual head. Spousals continued to be made *de futuro* and *de prœsenti*. Under the first the couple promised, or their parents for them if they were under the legal age, to marry sometime in the future unless circumstances should prevent. A vow taken *de prœsenti* was far more serious and might constitute a real marriage—to the extent at least that it could prevent either party from marrying another person. *Carnalis copula* was necessary to make the union complete in every respect before the law. The formal blessing of the church in a ceremony like the modern wedding was of secondary though increasing importance. The church had long insisted on the necessity of its participation in the spousal but, though the presence of a priest was usually sought when the vows were made, a simple plighting of troth by the two persons concerned was legally sufficient. Thus the legal position of women remained the same from 1527 to Cromwellian times. Shortly before Henry's death a commission met to alter the laws of marriage and divorce, and though their recommendations were rejected by Edward's commons they present the best opinion of the reformers and deserve mention here. They would allow a child who did not relish the choice of a spouse made by its parents to appeal to an ecclesiastical court for an action in restraint. Divorce should be granted for adultery and desertion, and where "violent hatred rendered it in the highest degree improbable that the husband and wife would survive their animosities and again love one another."[4] The rejection of this plan of reform marks a line of division; henceforth the Puritans sought to make marriage entirely a civil function and argued for absolute divorce. The divines of the established church were repeatedly called on to defend their official position and, in the case of Whitgift, felt the necessity of enforcing with the utmost rigidity the ecclesiastical law. The controversy over divorce becomes a part of the whole quarrel between prelatical episcopacy and presbytery.

[3] Some attempt was made to control this practice. Canon 107 (1603) is expressly aimed at it. "In all sentences pronounced only for divorce and separation *a thoro et a mensa*, there shall be a caution and restraint of the said sentence that the parties so separated shall live chastely and continently; neither shall they, during each other's life, contract matrimony with other persons."

[4] G. E. Howard, *A History of Matrimonial Institutions,* Chicago, 1904, II, pp. 78-79, presents the details of this far-sighted *Reformatio Legum Ecclesiasticorum.*

Friends of the Puritans are wont to point with satisfaction to this agitation for the reform of the divorce law as evidence of the high regard of the Puritan church for woman and the institution of marriage. Milton's view of the married state as a conjugal society of spiritual happiness and not a "prescribed satisfaction for irrational heat" seems to fortify their contentions. But the attitude toward mankind revealed in the sermons of Puritan and Anglican preachers are scarcely to be distinguished, as a brief examination of some of the statements made by members of both the high and the low church parties will show. Calvin held no very exalted idea of marriage. In the *Institutes* he describes it as a means of refuge from the consequences of sexual passion. Although he declares man was not created to live in solitude and that the Fall has made more necessary the presence of a help-meet for him, "the conjugal relation was ordained as a necessary means of preventing us from giving way to unbridled lust."[5] The great Latimer, defender of the oppressed husbandman, can say little more for womankind than the master of the Genevans: "But it is a part of your penance, ye women, to travail in bearing your children, so it is a part of your penance to be subjects unto your husbands; ye are underlings, underlings, and must be obedient."[6] Thomas Becon, the most popular preacher of the '60's, in his *Catechism* (a work which circulated widely) speaks more gently but no less firmly. The husband must be patient in dealing with his wife, "even such an one as a gentle and tender father is toward his most dear and sweet child, ever remembering that that sex . . . . is more weak in body and mind than the man is. . . . ."[7] Hooker sums up in the *Laws of Ecclesiastical Polity,* we may believe, the substance of hundreds of orthodox sermons:

> So that woman being created for man's sake to be his helper in regard to the end before mentioned, namely the having and the bringing up of children, whereunto it was not possible they could concur unless they were subalternation between them . . . . woman therefore was even in her first estate framed by nature not only after in time but inferior in excellency also unto man, howbeit in so due and sweet proportion as being presented before our eyes, might be sooner perceived than defined.[8]

The sentiments revealed in Donne's marriage sermons are strange indeed coming from the maker of many passionate love poems!

[5] *Institutes,* Edinburgh, 1845, I, p. 472.

[6] Last sermon preached before Edward VI. Parker Society edition, p. 253.

[7] *A New Catechism set forth dialogue-wise in familiar talk between the father and the son,* Parker Society Edition, p. 338.

[8] *Works,* collected in three volumes, Oxford, 1841, Book V, Ch. lxxiii, 3.

He is a miserable creature, whose creator is his wife. God did not stay to join her in commission with Adam, so far as to give names to the creatures; much less to give essence; essence to the man, essence to her husband. When the wife thinks her husband owes her all his fortune, all his discretion, all his reputation, God help that man himself, for he hath given him no helper yet. . . . . She was not taken out of the foot to be trodden upon, nor out of the head, to be overseer of him; but out of his side, where she weakens him enough and therefore should do all she can to be a helper.[9]

The arch-Puritan, Bunyan, in his *Christian Behaviour* lays down rules for wifely conduct and says, in reply to the *Objection*—"But my husband is a sot, a fool, and one that hath not wit enough to follow his outward employment in the world"—"Though all this be true, yet thou must know he is thy head. . . . . Wherefore, though in truth thou have more discretion than he, yet thou oughtest to know that thou, with all that is thine, art to be used as under thy husband, even in 'everything.' "[10]

The picture is not a pleasant one nor is it altogether easy to reconcile with the impression conveyed by the dramas written between 1595 and 1620. The popular domestic conduct books of the Tudor period are hardly more illuminating of actual conditions. They describe in minutest detail the obligations of wives, husbands, parents, and children but to read one is to read all. Becon's *New Catechism*, mentioned above, though strictly speaking not an example of the type, considers many of the usual problems in a delightful fashion and will serve as well as another to illustrate their general tone. It discusses at length the duties of wives and husbands, unmarried men, maids, and widows. The passage on the household occupations of the wife is too good to pass by:

The third point of a virtuous matron is to look unto her house . . . . to reprove vice sharply in her servants, and to commend virtue; not to meddle in other folks' business abroad, but diligently to look upon her own at home; not to go unto her neighbors' houses to tattle and prattle after the manner of light housewives; not to be tavern-hunters; not idly and wantonly to gad abroad, seeking new customers; not to resort unto places where common plays, interludes and pastimes be used; not to accompany herself with any light persons, but only with such as be sober, modest, grave, honest, godly, virtuous, housewifely, thrifty, of good name, well-reported and in fine, continually to remain at home in their house diligently and virtuously occupied, except urgent, weighty and necessary causes compel her to go forth, as to go unto the church to pray or to hear the

[9] *Works,* London, 1839, Vol. IV, Sermon lxxxii.
[10] *Works,* edited by Henry Stebbing, New York, Vol. II, p. 175.

word of God, to visit her sick neighbours or to help them, to go to the market to buy things necessary for her household. . . . . "[11]

The three kinds of evidence as to the position of woman in Elizabethan life thus far examined tell us only how the law and the church and the self-constituted regents of society proposed women should deport themselves. Anyone who has read Tudor biography possesses a surer guide to an understanding of the Elizabethan woman. Where in the canons, sermons, and books of conduct is there a place for such high-spirited ladies of the Queen's court as Ann Russell, Elizabeth Vernon, and Elizabeth Throckmorton? Thomas Becon and many another recommended that old widows give themselves entirely to the service of God, but Lady Magdalen Herbert preferred to settle in Oxford where she could keep an eye on her young hopeful, Edward, and at the same time enjoy the converse of the learned and virtuous members of the university. The actions of Sidney's Stella would not be sanctioned by a Hooker or a Whitgift. The foreigners who journeyed to England during these years are probably the safest witnesses. To a man they insist upon the liberty which English women enjoyed, in spite of the impression to the contrary of the foregoing pages.

Frederick, Duke of Wittemberg, whose memoirs were first printed in 1602, says they have more liberty than in any other place and know well how to make use of it.[12] Samuel Kiechel who arrived in 1585 found them accessible "and by nature so mighty pretty as I have scarcely ever beheld."[13] Visitors were particularly delighted with the English custom whereby the wife submits her cheek to a kiss from the newcomer, which mode of greeting Erasmus recommends as a good cure for the gout. A Hollander says significantly that though the women are entirely in the power of their husbands except for their lives, yet they are not kept so strictly as they are in Spain or elsewhere. They come and go as they please, leaving the household drudgery to their servants.

They sit before their doors, decked out in fine clothes, in order to see and be seen by the passers by. . . . . All the rest of their time they employ in walking and riding, in playing at cards or otherwise in visiting their friends and keeping company with their equals (whom they term gosseps) . . . . and making merry with them at child-births, christenings, churchings and funerals; and all with

[11] *New Catechism*, as above, p. 343.
[12] W. B. Rye, *England as Seen by Foreigners*, London, 1865, p. 7.
[13] *Ibid.*, p. 89.

the permission and knowledge of their husbands, as such is the custom. . . . . This is why England is called the Paradise of married women. . . . .[14]

It is no fortuitous circumstance that the woes and joys of women came to have an important place in Elizabethan drama. As these excerpts from the jottings of foreign visitors indicate, Tudor women, though supposedly the meek and pliant servants of their wedded husbands, in the eyes of the church mere weak vessels for the quenching of lust, actually enjoyed more liberty than their European sisters. In the great days of the drama they went with their husbands to the public playhouses, or if they were ladies and such was unseemly, the actors came to court or played for them in private theaters where the vulgar eye could not stare at their loveliness. Their tastes and their troubles had to be considered by a playwright who would be popular.

II

THE ABUSED WIFE

The great Christian virtues are patience and meekness, qualities especially desirable in the female of the human species. The Middle Ages relished tales exemplifying these virtues as the collection of legends known as the Constance-Griselda-Florence cycle proves. The theme of the long-suffering wife, successor to the earlier story of the woman saint who bears all for the Lord's sake, came to be one of the most popular in the stock of the medieval story-teller. In Germany between 1470 and 1527 Griselda made twelve appearances.[15] Chaucer had received her in England a hundred years previously. The Italian novel writers of the sixteenth century delighted in the tales of calumniated wives—whence the plots of *James IV, Othello,* and *Much Ado.* One is not surprised, on this account, to find the woes of abused or slandered matrons a frequent subject with the Elizabethan dramatists, particularly during the years when the medieval influence was still powerful and plays were written about typical and recurrent situations. The number and the success of these plays, moreover, testifies to the lingering belief that the drama should be an instrument of morality.

John Phillips' *Commodye of pacient and meeke Grissill* (c. 1565), already discussed as an example of the transitional morality, inaugurates

---

[14] Rye, pp. 72-73.

[15] Franz Falk, "Die Ehe am Ausgang des Mittelalters," p. 45. (In *Janssen's Geschichte des deutschen Volkes,* herausgegeben von Ludwig Pastor, Freiburg, 1908, Vol. VI.)

a series of more than twenty extant plays dealing with the sorrows of injured wives. The author follows Boccaccio closely, allowing himself, however, the liberty of adding a complete outfit of morality figures and inserting "moral matter" especially concerned with the rearing of children. He shows a slight sense for dramatic values in the invention of Persuasion, a councillor whose business it is to suggest the trial of Grissill. The heroine is withal so very patient that one doubts whether she has wit enough to be otherwise.

Robert Greene is the first of the professional dramatists who attempts the theme of the distressed wife. Queen Dorothea in *James IV* comes to mind at once, a heroine and a play born, as it were, before their time for in theme and treatment *James IV* is allied with the popular reconciliation dramas of the next century and as well with the tragi-comedy of Beaumont and Fletcher. A less-known heroine of Greene's, Angelica, in *Orlando Furioso,* deserves mention. Through the machinations of the villain, Sacripant, Orlando is made to believe his betrothed lady has proved false to her profession of love. He abandons her, goes mad with grief and persists in his delusion until the enchantress Melissa tells him of the deception. Eventually the lovers are united and all ends merrily. That Angelica regards Orlando as her husband is clear from her references to him; she calls him Lord although a formal wedding has not yet taken place. Greene did not find this story ready at hand. In Ariosto's poem the heroine is really in love with Medoro and eventually marries him instead of Orlando. The theme of the calumniated and deserted maid-wife is, therefore, Greene's own variation on the original story. In order to piece out the last scenes of *Friar Bacon* he once more makes use of the stock situation, though in this instance the victim, Margaret, is not accused of wrongdoing when her husband abandons her. She and Lacy, it will be remembered, are making a spousal *de præsenti* before Friar Bungay while the Prince and Bacon look on through a magic "prospective glass."   Bacon, in the midst of the ceremony, charms the priest into silence. But the betrothal is valid for Lacy says:

> . . . . what he cannot with his book,
> We'll twixt us both unite it up in heart.

Later Prince Edward magnanimously yields his suit to Margaret and all seems settled for the pair. But Greene is at a loss to keep the love-story going while he finishes the Bacon plot. So Lacy sends his espoused a letter repudiating her for no apparent reason.[16] Margaret is about to enter a convent when Lacy rides up to tell her his act was planned merely "to try sweet Peggy's constancy." With little demuring she is pursuaded to doff her nun's robes and pardon him. We are inclined to wonder at the regularity with which betrayed women like Margaret enter convents. But what else can they do? They are married in the eyes of the law and may not make another attempt. The only divorce possible is a separation without the privilege of remarriage. Plays like *Friar Bacon* illustrate the domestic code discussed in the beginning of this chapter.[17]

The Pleasant Comedie of Patient Grissil, written by Dekker, Chettle, and Haughton, entered on the Register in March of 1600 and acted sometime the previous autumn, seems to have been responsible for a vogue of patient-wife plays which continued for half-a-dozen years. It is an honest attempt to give dramatic values to the old story. In characteristic Elizabethan fashion the authors have enriched the plot by the addition of a contrasted theme of the taming of a shrewish wife. The play becomes then a kind of homily on the ruling of wives. The harshness of the original story has been much softened. The cruel husband is at times so moved by his own cruelty that he can scarcely continue the torturing. His servants weep in the performance of their disagreeable tasks. The various trials Grissil is made to endure are not inflicted without some apology; following the suggestion in Boccaccio the authors make the Marquis excuse himself on the ground that his people are angry because he has married a poor girl without a family. One dramatic device deserves particular mention. A kind of chorus character in the person of Lucio, Grissil's brother, is provided to

[16] The test of constancy is, of course, a favorite in the ballads, as in *Child Waters,* for example.

[17] The case of Queen Isabella in Marlowe's *Edward II,* though more properly discussed, perhaps, in another category, presents some interesting considerations. In Holinshed Marlowe found dimly outlined the story of a distressed wife whose patience finally breaks under the strain. The historian makes much of this ultimate infidelity. Marlowe omits any moral observations although he alters history to the extent of suggesting that death may be the punishment for her complicity in the murder of Edward whereas in actual fact Isabella lived a peaceful and even luxurious life after the murder of her husband. It would seem—in spite of critical opinion to the contrary—as if Marlowe had tried in this instance to explore the recesses of the feminine mind. The theme of the injured wife he developed from the slightest hints in the source; the transformation of character though not sufficiently developed is none the less indicated.

speak for the audience in voicing the resentment they are bound to feel for the wanton treatment his sister receives. The play is especially noteworthy because it attempts to bring the story of the abused wife out of the realm of romance and endow it with real instead of traditional emotions. Its immediate successors draw even closer to life.

The next play on this long list, *How a Man May Choose a Good Wife from a Bad,* enjoyed phenomenal popularity if seven reprintings in thirty years may be considered significant. Although the source is Italian[18] the author has domesticated the plot. Young Arthur, grown tired of his wife, leaves her bed for that of a "great courtesan" and eventually administers her a dose of poison in order that he may marry his mistress. But the poison, as usual in Italian stories, is only a sleeping potion, and the distressed wife wakes up in her tomb. The wicked husband is betrayed by his new wife and the law is about to punish him for murder when his faithful spouse turns up in court where a reconciliation takes place and the moral is made plain to the audience. All this the source supplies. Note how it has been Anglicized. The fathers of the couple interfere in their domestic difficulties in a vain attempt to bring the erring husband to a reformation. They even take the case before a judge and beg him to give their son some useful instruction since he scorns their advice. The judge betrays little interest-in the case; in fact he does not even take the trouble to discover which party is at fault. We can forgive the author for his failure to motivate Young Arthur's actions since he has, in these preliminary scenes, taken us inside a middle-class home and shown us a genuine domestic squabble of the year 1600. It is possible that this play inspired the anonymous author of *The Faire Maide of Bristowe* to emulation. At least there are more points of similarity between these two plays than is the case with any others in this group of reconciliation dramas. Again the husband's wanton treatment of his wife—this time he does not succeed in his plan to poison her, for the plot is revealed and he is driven out by her father—received no motivation. Yet the story, once this romantic premise is granted, unrolls with gratifying vividness. By a trick Vallenger (the prodigal husband) is charged with the murder of one of his mistress' suitors. The wife remains faithful even through this trial and endeavors to take his place on the scaffold. Fortunately the supposedly murdered man comes to

[18] Deca Terza, Novella V, Cinthio's *Hecatommithi*. Swaen in his edition (*Materialen* 35) argues for Riche's translation as the immediate source.

life, the poison once more proving to be only a soporific. There is turn and turn about at repenting; husband and wife fall into each other's arms and the courtesan, now providentially reformed by the sight of so much virtue in the world, enters a convent to expiate her many sins. Intrinsically the play is not the equal of the earlier *How a Man may Choose;* historically it has significance because, so far as we know, the plot is the invention of the author and the mise en scène, except for the negligible fact that the magistrate who adjudges the case in Act V is Richard I, is entirely contemporary.[19] In other words the source of inspiration is not bookish although many of the situations might easily have been pilfered from the common store-house to which all Elizabethan dramatists had a pass-key.[20]

The London Prodigal (printed 1605) is unique for several reasons. Although it belongs to the general group under discussion, it has shaken off most of the devices of Italian romance and stands alone as one of the first naturalistic dramas in English. Moreover it so nearly approaches in theme and tone the sentimental drama of the eighteenth century that the very real differences between it and the later plays on the same subject are not instantly apparent. The setting is contemporary London. A father, giving out that he has died abroad, disguises himself, enters the employ of his prodigal son and proceeds to manage his affairs. He arranges a marriage for him with the virtuous daughter of Sir Lancelot Spurcock but becomes so disgusted with his son's mercenary attitude toward the match that he causes him to be arrested for debt on his wedding day, hoping that this calamity may bring him to terms. The prodigal is deserted by all save his faithful wife, but her sacrifice does not alter in the least his riotous course. He blasphemes the memory of his father, casts off his faithful servant, tries to filch from his wife the pittance which a compassionate uncle had given her and finally casts her off with:

> . . . . turn whore, thats a good trade,
> And so perhaps ile see thee now and then.

[19] Collier properly rejected the possibility that the play derived from the ballad of "Maudlin, the Merchant's Daughter of Bristol."

[20] If, as it seems likely, the author of the *Fair Maid* is indebted to Marston's *Dutch Courtesan* for the detail of the plot whereby Blunt is commanded by the courtesan to murder his friend Sentloe, whom she wishes out of the way that she may enjoy Vallenger undisturbed, we have additional evidence of his emancipation from the use of purely literary source materials. Baskerville discusses this question of influence in *P.M.L.A.*, xxiv, p. 711 ff.

In the end she is the means of saving his life.[21] Her father intends
to prosecute him for murder since she is not to be found, but her appearance at the right moment prevents his arrest. A complete reconciliation takes place and the prodigal is reformed. Because this
moving scene is made the more joyful by the promise of a large dowry
and the prospect of material blessings for the re-betrothed pair, an
inevitable accompaniment to most eighteenth century dramas of re-
generation, some have been inclined to call this play a genuine sentimental drama. This important difference is to be noted. Sentimental
drama as it was known in its great day—and that day has not yet
altogether declined—assumed the fundamental goodness of human
nature as a postulate. Sin became, therefore, an aberration resulting
from evil counsel or ignorance. But the Elizabethans were far from
being Rousseauists. This particular sinner is pictured from the beginning as a thoroughly depraved young man, utterly wanting in any
tender feeling or natural affection. His reformation comes as a kind
of baptism, a giving over of the sins of the world by the aid of the
regenerative power of his wife's virtue. The beast of original sin within
him has, as it were, been slain.

George Wilkins' *Miseries of Enforced Marriage* which followed
the *London Prodigal* after two years may well represent the climax
of this series. It dispenses with disguises and all romantic machinery
and tells a pitiful story to illustrate the thesis which the author makes
plain in his title. Wilkins was not the first to plead for more humane
provisions about contract marriage. The literature on marriage and
divorce written during the previous century frequently urges parents to
consult the wishes of the minors under their charge. The commission
of 1552 recommended, it will be remembered, that they be compelled
to do so. The case of young Scareborrow is anomalous. Since he is
eighteen he can legally contract to marry whom he chooses—as he
does soon after the play begins. But his guardian has meantime
found him another wife and arranged a match. He possesses power
to force the marriage in spite of the fact that his ward becomes an
adulterer thereby and both the wife of his choice and Katherine, whom
his guardian has selected, are made whores. From this distressful

---

[21] Sir Lancelot has already threatened to bring suit for divorce, as he legally
may since the prodigal deceived him in regard to his financial status. Again, as in
How a Man May Choose, the wife's patience is intensified by her refusal to take
advantage of a situation which would free her from the sinner she has married
and allow her to make another trial.

situation Wilkins constructs a play as apposite for his time as *A Doll's House* was in the 1880's. The deserted Clare through love of her wronged husband dies by her own hand to save his soul from the stain of adultery.

> I'll be a wife now, help to save his soul
> Though I have lost his body; give a slake
> To his iniquities, and with one sin,
> Done by this hand, end many done by him. . . . .
> Yet record world, though an act too foul,
> A wife thus died, to cleanse her husband's soul.[22]

Scareborrow, moved to bitterness by the sacrifice, resolves never to love or cherish the wife who has been forced upon him. She is made to endure all things until the guardian providentially dies, acknowledging the evil he has done and endowing his ward with wealth sufficient to replace all he has lost during his prodigal days. The author patches up a sentimental ending and forgiveness is passed freely about. For the first time among all these plays the patient wife actually meets death. Odd that the frequent repetition of this motif should thus far yield only one tragedy and even that a strange hybrid which ends in the conventional fashion. But the fact betrays the attitude of the dramatists toward the problem of a wife's loyalty. Although the later plays are conceived with considerable attention to the motivation of the husband's cruelty and frequently succeed in making the wife articulate and not merely a passive sufferer, in nearly every instance the moral import is the same: the wife whose steadfastness under trial never falters is certain of justification in the end.

In the light of the present discussion *A Yorkshire Tragedy* (1608) assumes significance apart from its importance as one of the most stirring of the domestic tragedies based on contemporary events. In it the woes of the injured but patient and forgiving wife receive a large share of the author's attention. As a matter of historical fact the wife was herself not altogether an unstained saint; yet her rôle in the play is developed in the tradition established by the other dramas of this type. At the very end she still persists in the hope that pardon may be pronounced, and the "Master of a College" concludes with lines referring to her virtues:

> Was it in man to woond so kinde a creature?
> Ile ever praise a woman for thy sake. . . . .

[22] Hazlitt's Dodsley, IX, p. 502.

Not all the abused wives of Elizabethan drama endured their husband's wanton behavior without retaliation. History obliged Marlowe to bring Isabella's patience to an end and there are others, less culpable perhaps, who can keep her company. Sometime between 1596 and 1600 a curious gallimaufry of romantic left-overs, *The Wisdom of Doctor Doddipoll,* was served up to the London stage. The main-plot is concerned with enchantments, potions, falling in love, and giving in marriage; the sub-plot is the story of a maid betrothed to a court painter by a private spousal. Their loves are rudely exposed and marriage is forced upon them. The new husband conceives an instant dislike for the wife he previously adored and tries to rid himself of her. But she insists on following him about. At last she is persuaded, by her friends, to desert him and go back to the court where he eventually turns up for a reconciliation, laconically expressed in the lines:

> . . . . since her departure I have done
> More hartie penance than her hart could wish,
> And vowe hereafter to live ever hers.

Heywood's *Wise Woman of Hogsdon* furnishes the best example, outside Shakespeare, of the wronged maiden-wife who forces her erring spouse to a right-about. Briefly the story is as follows. Chartley, "a wild-headed gentleman," deserts his betrothed Luce, comes up to London, and is married secretly to another woman of the same name whom he deserts in turn for an heiress. The injured country-girl meantime has not been idly twiddling her thumbs at home. She follows him to London and by a scheme contrived at the establishment of the Wise Woman gets Chartley bound to her more firmly than by the private spousal he has renounced. His secret marriage to the second Luce takes place in the dark and he really marries his first affianced wife while his intended bride becomes the wife of an ardent suitor of hers who is party to the plot. When all is made plain in the last scene, the prodigal reforms in short order and the three couples— for the heiress has found a husband—are left by the author on this side the paradise of married life.

The conduct of Infelice in Dekker's *Honest Whore II,* though more sinister as befits the tone of the play, is quite as spirited as that of Luce. It will be remembered that Hippolito whose harsh words and high morality in the first part of the play had wrought the reform of Bellafront, falls from grace and tempts her in the second

part to cuckold Matheo who married her to make her an honest
woman. Infelice, Hippolito's fine-tempered wife, learns of his behaviour through Bellafront's father who brings her the love-letters, a
purse, and a ring (her own trinkets, more's the pity) with which
Hippolito had tried to compass his wooing. The injured lady faces
her lord with his shameless act in a splendid scene of mingled rage and
irony but she cannot move him to repentance. In the last act she
demands justice be done on Bellafront for she believes her guilty of
the alienation of her husband's affections. He rises to her defence,
declares her an honest wife for all of him, and Infelice must perforce
be satisfied. One observes with pleasure that Dekker is too much
of an artist to patch up an elaborate reconciliation either in this
or in the main plot of the play where the prodigal Matheo is brought
to his knees. Dekker's portrait-gallery of injured women includes
the Queen in his Beaumontesque tragi-comedy *Match Me in London*
(?1612). Her royal spouse has brought to court Tormiella, a trades-
man's wife, and is endeavoring to make her his mistress. The Queen
by no means endures the slight in silence. She taunts him with ironic
speeches, reviles his innocent prey, and even plans an attempt on her
life. When she learns, however, from poor Tormiella how loathsome
the King's actions are to her, she melts and forgives:

> . . . . We both ith field being wounded,
> Since we must needs be sharers, use me kindly. . . . .

The conventions of tragi-comedy demand that the King shall put away his
wife and try to murder her, with the inevitable outcome that she does
not die but, like Hermione, is eventually reconciled to her husband.

It will be observed that Shakespeare allies himself with the writers
who make injured wifehood articulate. Desdemona is an exception,
it is true, but Desdemona's patience does not save her life. Hero
collapses under the blow of calumny but her weakness only makes
Beatrice's resentment the more notable. One of the finest and truest
speeches in the whole body of Shakespeare's work is Hermione's
dignified and queenly defense of her honour. It burns like a brand-
ing iron and Paulina's frenzied vituperation, reminiscent of Emilia's
rage, heaped upon Leontes, is nothing to it. Queen Katherine speaks
in the same vein in words of Shakespeare's writing and when Justice
is blinded in her presence she sweeps out of the court-room with the
proud lines:

> Now the Lord help!
> They vex me past my patience. Pray you, pass on,

> I will not tarry, no, nor ever more
> Upon this business my appearance make
> In any of their courts. (II, 4, 127-131)

The injured Imogen wastes no time in soft repining. The word "false" uttered by perplexed Pisanio stings her to cry out:

> False to his bed! What! is it false
> To lie in watch there and think on him;
> To weep 'twixt clock and clock; if sleep change nature,
> To break it with a fearful dream of him
> And cry myself awake? That's false to's bed is it? (III, 3, 42-46)

She so belabours the fellow with taunts, because coward-like he refuses to obey his master and dispatch her, that he can scarcely control his wits. Helena is, of course, the most determined of Shakespeare's abused wives.

I have saved for the last a word about three interesting treatments of the theme of the distressed wife, all by major dramatists: Bellafront in the *Honest Whore II* (1604), Celia in *Volpone* (1605), and Isabella in the *White Devil* (1611). Bellafront in Part One, as noted above, contrived to force her betrayer, Matheo, to make her an honest woman. He yields with all the grace he can command but we are none too sure the match will prove to be ideal. In the second part he becomes the conventional prodigal husband, with this difference, that her past life recurs to vex him whenever his present difficulties are unbearable. To her woes is added this constant resentment which is fanned into raging flame when he suspects Hippolito has used his bed. In Bellafront Dekker succeeds in creating what is to my mind the most realistic figure in Elizabethan drama. For a whore to marry a gentleman and be made respectable is not an unusual thing in this drama[23] and was probably not uncommon in Elizabethan life but no other playwright set himself the task of analyzing the anguish of a woman whom the world will not allow to reform. Although the play is technically a study of the distressed wife, it possesses significance as a study developed in no conventional manner, in the aftermath of the evils which men do and the consequences which live after their conversion.

The episode of Celia and her wicked husband in *Volpone* is an interesting use of the old theme in the larger scheme of that savage,

[23] There comes to mind Doll in *Northward Hoe* and the country girl in *Michaelmas Term,* who is married by the man who has been keeping her. Young Follywit in *A Mad World My Masters* is tricked into marriage by a courtesan.

Swiftian comedy. Jonson poured all his concentrated hate of shameless men into the arguments Corvino uses to force his wife to Volpone's
will. Her impotent anguish before the villainy of her husband and the
lust of Volpone would move even a saint to blasphemy. The author
gives her justice in the end after rescuing her by means of Bonario.
She is sent back to her father with a trebled dowry.

The pitiful story of Isabella whom Brachiano deserts and murders
for the sake of the White Devil presents at least one variation on the
old theme and demands attention for the penetration with which
Webster writes the great scene of the poor wife's story. She has followed her husband to Rome and meets him there. Their words of
greeting show instantly that all love has died within him though he
speaks with cruel restraint. To her piteous request for a kiss he replies:

> I do not use to kiss:
> If that will dispossess your jealousy
> I'll swear it to you.[24]

She tries to embrace him. Here is the touch, disagreeable but infallible,
which is worth many a scene in the plays we have been studying:

> *Brachiano* O, your breath!
>   Out upon sweetmeats and continued physic,—
>   The plague is in them.
> *Isabella*   You have oft, for those two lips,
>   Neglected cassia or the natural sweets
>   Of the spring violet: they are not yet much withered.[25]

How much is told of days past in these few lines! Again in the resolution of this scene there is a touch of genius. Isabella, without
heroics, offers to work peace between her husband and her powerful
brother, the Duke:

> . . . . I will make
> Myself the author of your cursed vow;
> I have some cause to do, you have none,
>   . . . . let the fault
> Remain with my supposed jealousy;
> And think with what a piteous and rent heart
> I shall perform this sad ensuing part.

And in the next scene she acts the virago, in her pretended rage.
There is no anguish quite like it in all the plays before or since, save

[24] II, 1, p. 27, Mermaid edition.
[25] II, 1, p. 28, Mermaid edition.

in the *Broken Heart* when Calantha dances on though her heart is laden with woe for the deaths of her lover, her father, and Penthea.[26]

It is time to cast up accounts and estimate the significance of this study of the abused wife as regards the general problem of the Elizabethan drama and morality. Several facts are evident: the theme was popular, especially on the more public stages;[27] it shows itself first in a romantic setting which is soon abandoned for a contemporary mise en scène and an English cast of characters; the dramatists soon discover its usefulness in making a sub-plot or providing contrasts. Usually the moral is all too-well pointed as in *How a Man may Choose a Good Wife*, for example, where Young Arthur, standing between the wife he tried to poison and the courtesan who tried to effect his death, admonishes the audience with a homily on marriage. This didactic element, present as a matter of course in most of the plays of the series, must have gratified an audience which had for years been taught to look to the drama for moral instruction.[28] On

---

[26] It occurs to me that Beaumont and Fletcher may have adapted from the popular stage the theme of the injured maiden-wife in the *Maid's Tragedy* and *A King and No King*. It is true that neither Aspatia nor Spaconia is a wedded wife but the first has had a promise of marriage and the latter says of her relations with Tigranes:

> . . . . as fast
> As oaths without a formal ceremony
> Can make him, I am to him. (II, 303-306)

[27] Shakespeare's company performed, in addition to his own plays with this plot, *The London Prodigal, The Miseries of Enforced Marriage, A Yorkshire Tragedy*, and *The Faire Maide of Bristowe*. To Henslowe's Company belonged the *Patient Grissil* and *The Honest Whore*. Heywood wrote for the Earl of Worcester's company (later Queen Anne's Men) which presumably owned his *Wise Woman* as they did *How a Man May Choose a Good Wife*. Each of the great companies apparently felt the need of having such plays in its repertoire.

The list, by the way, is by no means exhausted though the important exemplars of the type have been treated . For completeness' sake there should be added Brandon's *Octavia*, the *Death of Robert, Earl of Huntington* (the Queen whom John forsakes in his lust for Matilda), *Fair Em* (the case of Em and Manvile), *Satiromastix* (Caelistine), *Lust's Dominion* (Maria), *Alphonsus, Emperor of Germany* (the Empress), Heywood's *Royal King and Loyal Subject* (the Queen).

[28] The Marquis in the later *Patient Grissil* delivers a short sermon of eight lines on the trying of a wife (2921-2929). The Father in the *London Prodigal* lectures his son—after his reform—on the dangers of backsliding. The didactic quality of the *Miseries of Enforced Marriage* is sufficiently indicated by the synopsis given above but it abounds in moral passages. Bellafront in the *Honest Whore II* discourses at length on the miserable life of whores and courtesans.

the other hand one notes a gradual drawing nearer to life and a desire to interpret the situations devised, not in accord with the literary tradition or authoritarian standards, but as a knowledge of human actions requires. This change modern philosophers would say is in the direction of a higher morality for it indicates a conscious attack on ethical problems. Finally the plays supplement what we know of Elizabethan woman from the provisions of the law and the preachments of the church. There is little talk of divorce in this drama; seldom is there recourse to the law. Women did possess inalienable rights as we see when a renegade, newly espoused husband yields gracefully after his determined maid-wife tricks him into an acknowledgement of the contract he has made. The spousal could be made binding and husbands could be forced to keep their wedding vows but the law and the church apparently left the matter in the hands of the individuals concerned. Evidently patience was a virtue any Elizabethan woman had good need of and these stories, extravagant as many of them seem to us, may perhaps reflect life more than we should be inclined to suspect.

III

THE FAITHFUL WIFE

Thomas Becon, like all other moralists, admits a great fear of that "pestiferous mermaid, the flesh." For the good wife he has a particular word of caution. Let her, he says in the *New Catechism,* have an eye out for the devil who comes as a roaring lion seeking to entice her to defile her husband's marriage bed. Elizabethan dramatists, however, had little use for the roaring lion unless he succeeded in devouring his prey. Yet he appears in a few of the plays previously discussed to distress the already sufficiently perplexed wife. Mistress Arthur in *How a Man May Choose a Good Wife,* for example, repulses the wicked advances of Anselm who pursues even into the tomb where on waking she finds him ready with more arguments. But her steadfastness turns him and he brings her to his mother's house and protects her until her difficulties are resolved. The Honest Whore is forced to endure a siege from the man who had effected her conversion. He finally gives over the struggle and clears her honesty. A variation on the theme of the tempted wife which possessed great theatric value is the story of the chaste woman importuned by her sovereign to commit adultery with him. If Greene wrote the *Pinner of Wakefield,* it may be that he is responsible for the vogue. One of the by-plots of the play shows Jane-a-Barley resisting the evil desires of King James. He rides up when her husband is away and tries to force her to open the castle to him by threatening to kill her son if she will not yield. She is prepared to sacrifice her child rather than her honour but old Musgrove arrives providentially and brings James to a better mind about the matter. The fortitude of Jane is equalled by the Countess of Salisbury's repulse of another royal wooer, Edward III, in the play of that name. The King tries every means in his power short of physical violence to force her honour; he even promises to put out of the way his own queen and the Countess' husband, to swim a Hellespont of blood, "to aryve at Cestus where my Hero lies." She seems to yield, then turns upon him with a fine gesture, displays two daggers, gives him one to use upon his queen if he will, and swears unless he desists,

> . . . . this sharp pointed knyfe
> Shall staine thy earth with that which thou would staine,
> My poore chast blood.

The King is instantly cured of his lust. He praises her virtue and promises never to trouble her more. The author of this history—there is some reason to believe Shakespeare is to be discovered in this portion—got no hint for the episode of the royal wooing from Holinshed but has adapted to his uses a tale from Painter's *Palace of Pleasure* (xlvi) in order to fill out and enliven the chronicle of Edward's French and Scottish wars.[29]

A curious version of this motif of a king's lust for his subject's wife occurs in Dekker's *Satiromastix,* a play evidently hastily made up for use as ammunition in the War of the Theaters. The romantic sub-structure on which the satiric material has been placed concerns the wicked love of William Rufus for the bride of Sir Walter Terrell. The ever-useful sleeping potion furnishes a solution and Caelistine is carried before the King as dead. Of course the husband and the wife are not aware that the cup does not contain a deadly poison. Such a betrayal of the law of suspense would never do. Otherwise the husband could not rage against his sovereign so resoundingly in the

---

[29] The play differs from the novel in the important particular that the Countess is not pictured as a widow and rewarded for her proper behaviour with marriage to the king.

last act and the King's contrition at the bier would lose its savour. Caelistine's chastity is a mechanic thing and she is generally so acquiescent that many a lesser man than Dekker might have created her.[30] But her story is interesting as a precursor of the kind of drama Beaumont and Fletcher would make popular. Nearly contemporary with *Satiromastix* is Heywood's *Rape of Lucrece*. The episode which forms the center of the play is actually only one of five elements in the whole plot which aside from the lamentable story of Lucrece is really a Roman Chronicle History. She first appears reproving her housemaids for immodest behaviour, and there is generally a touch of the English matron about her. Heywood, being a writer of domestic tragedies for bourgeois audiences, has inevitably vulgarized the tale.

The omnipresent potion aids Maria in that most passion-rending murder play, *Lust's Dominion or the Lascivious Queen*. This poor wife is sought by her King and though her husband is the paramour of the Queen Mother and thinks to use her as a means of climbing to greater heights, she resists faithfully until the audience begins to fear a repetition of Tarquin's crime. But Fernando is no Tarquin though he has dragged her from her lonely bed and holds a dagger threateningly. He will do murder on himself, he declares, if she will not submit. A new development of an old situation! She remembers the useful drug in time to save his life and he falls asleep just as he hopes to embrace her. The court rushes in and the Queen Mother, seeing her son apparently murdered, kills Maria. In the discussion of the abused wife mention was made of the tragi-comedy *Match Me in London*. Though 'tis a poor thing Dekker manages to variegate the old theme by the introduction of a wicked lady-bawd, who entices Tormiella from her husband's shop, and by the distressed wife's simulated madness whereby she hopes to rid herself of the King's attentions. She is resolved to kill her oppressor rather than consummate a marriage with him—which becomes possible after the supposed murder of the Queen. A warning from heaven in the guise of stage thunder brings him to a pause, and in short order Tormiella·is restored to her raging but powerless husband.

This bead-roll of plays about the virtuous wife yields little.[31] One

[30] Caelistine has a place among the distressed wives. Sir Walter urges her to go to the King for he has sworn an oath that she shall go to the court on her wedding night.

[31] A few examples have been left aside. When the heroic plays were in vogue captured wives had ever to be wary lest some shameless conqueror do them wrong.

finds no line of development, no striking figures aside from the Countess of Salisbury and the Honest Whore.   The fact is that the theme has slight dramatic value save for an effective scene or two.   A play cannot be built on it unless the plot is eked out by all manner of devices such as Dekker uses in *Match Me in London.*   Nor does one learn much about Elizabethan women from these plays for in no instances aside from those of Bellafront and of Mistress Arthur does the motif move out of the realm of history or romance.   When we come to consider, as we shall presently, the tempted wife who succumbs to the invitation of her tempter, there will be another story to tell.

IV

DISTRESSED MAIDENS

It is curious that in the Elizabethan plays presenting the sorrows of womankind, distressed maidens should have so much less prominent a place than distressed wives.   This may well represent an actual condition in Elizabethan life.   It will be remembered that visitors to England during this period agree that wives have more liberty there (and are therefore in greater danger of temptation) than their European sisters, while the maidens are kept closely at home.[32]   Moreover it is often difficult in the plays to distinguish the exact status of the women concerned.   Technically a marriage was not completed after a spousal until bodily union had taken place or the church had given its formal blessing.   The girl ought still to be called maid and not wife, though we have already noted instances where this is not observed.   In any case she might properly no longer permit the "accost" of another suitor and to yield to a seducer meant adultery and not fornication.   In the following short discussion, with one exception,

---

In the *Wars of Cyrus* the captive Queen Panthea is besought for favors by the Persian Araspes.   All else failing he engages a magician to charm her to a capitulation but to no effect.   She demands justice from Cyrus who promises to reprimand his lewd and ungentlemanly subject.   Panthea, full of gratitude, sends for her husband to come to the aid of Cyrus.   More tragic is the fate of Olympia in the second part of *Tamburlaine* and of Perseda in *Soliman and Perseda.*

Maria *(Antonio's Revenge)*, a kind of virtuous Queen Gertrude, should not be forgotten.

[32] Van Meteren says: The girls who are not yet married are kept much more rigorously and strictly than in the Low Countries.   Rye, p. 75.

only those maidens will find a place who appear to be considered such by their eulogizers.

The first uncorruptable maiden in the English drama was born in Spain—Melibea in the tragi-comedy of *Calisto and Melibea,* an interlude showing the "Beauty and Good Properties of Women." The "old quean (and) bawdy witch" Celestina has all but brought her to Calisto's arms when a dream of her father shows her the danger ahead and she draws away from sin. The English reviser altered his original wantonly in the interests of morality, for the Spanish heroine succumbs and the story ends in calamity. A sad tale of a forced maid occurs in *Cambises.* This cruel tyrant compels his cousin-german to marry him against her will though she protests that such a crime is a thing that nature's course "doth utterly detest." Among the pre-Shakespearean heroines Virginia deserves the first place. Her sad story, contained in *A New Tragicall Comedie of Apius and Virginia,* was intended as a warning and an exhortation but possesses some real merits as a work of art.

Robert Greene was an innovator in this domain as elsewhere in the drama of troubled womankind. Margaret of Fressingfield refuses the unlawful love of a prince and Countess Ida welcomes a match with Eustace to escape the criminal wooing of King James. Another member of the romantic school, Anthony Munday, created perhaps the most unfortunate maiden on the Elizabethan stage—Matilda in the *Death of Robert Earl of Huntington.* Again we encounter a maid-wife for she has espoused Robert who dies in the first act of the play. But the lovers have been very careful about their conduct. Doncaster sneers at Robert's rectitude:

> . . . . he keeps a paltry, whindling girl,
> And will not bed her, forsooth before he bride. . . . .

Salisbury calls her "maiden fair," "virgin spouse," "poor chaste child." After Robert's death her life becomes unendurable because of the base suit of King John. Her flight to a nunnery to escape him avails nothing for the abbess is a bawd and works for her undoing. In consequence she receives with delight the poison Brand is commanded to give her if she will not yield. Munday obviously belongs with the moralists for the play preaches more fervidly against lust than a camp-meeting exhorter. Yet the conclusion equivocates. The revolting barons, ready to depose John for his cruelty, decide that a hastily

reformed English villain is a better bet than an untried French prince
and he is parolled, so to speak, during good behaviour.

The resolute honesty of Castizia furnishes some of the best scenes
in the *Revenger's Tragedy* (S. R. 1607). Her brother Vendice, disguised, pretends to play the bawd for Lussurioso but is overjoyed
when she sends him back to his master with ears well boxed. His
interview with their mother, however, results in her promise to change
Castizia's mind. This wicked promise gives occasion later for a fine
theatric scene in which Vendice and his brother threaten her with
death and bring her to repentance. Castizia now appears, seemingly
won over by her mother's previous seductive pleading. But this is
all a trick and the scene ends in the reconciliation of the two women
and a set speech on chastity by the heroine:

> . . . . no tongue has force
> To alter me from honest.
> If maidens would, men's words could have no power;
> A virgin's honour is a crystal tower
> Which (being weak) is guarded with good spirits;
> Until she yields, no ill inherits.[33]

Beaumont and Fletcher exploited the sorrows of distressed maids
to a far greater extent than any of their predecessors.[34] They especially delighted in the invention of situations from which no escape to
happiness was possible. Thus Aspatia, the technical heroine of the
Maid's Tragedy, can hope for no redress since her beloved is com-

---

[33] p. 418, Mermaid edition.

[34] The most striking example of all Elizabethan plays with chastity as their
subject is, of course, Fletcher's *Faithful Shepherdess*. Altogether too much deep
thought has been wasted on it, to my mind; not that it lacks merit, for few
plays of the period contain such melodious verse, but merely because it is not a
play to be taken seriously. It is clear from the following lines (to the Reader)
that he wishes to place himself in the tradition of *literary* pastoralism. "Understand, therefore, a pastoral to be a representation of shepherds and shepherdesses
with their actions and passions, which must be such as agree with their natures,
at least *not exceeding former fictions and vulgar traditions.*" (Italics mine). In
other words, it seems to me, Fletcher purposes writing a play in the best pastoral,
that is to say, an artificial manner. It happened that the praise of chastity and
the idealization of spiritual love were among the conventional materials of the
literary pastoral and consequently found a place in his poem. His work is no
more to be judged by realistic standards than is the *Faerie Queene* or *Comus*. The
failure of the play (1608) shows that the great age of the realistic drama was not
yet over. The time would soon come when plays dealing in an artificial fashion
with the problems of sex would be popular with the ever-narrowing circle of
theater-goers but that time was not yet arrived.

manded by the King to marry another. Euphrasia follows Philaster in disguise, receives unmerited wounds from him without a murmur and in the end refuses a husband, preferring "to serve the princess, to see the virtues of her lord and her." Spaconia in *A King and No King* is only restored to her Tigranes through the same happy accident which opens a way out of the labyrinth in which Arbaces and Panthea are wandering. In only one instance—the story of Ricardo and Viola in the *Coxcomb*—do we find a tale of love told in the realistic manner; there was no more delightful drama of reconciliation written during these years. It is an odd fact that these two authors, who create a world where men rule and women suffer, should also be among the originators of the comedy of manners where, as Meredith observes, the first necessity is the equality of the sexes.

V

The Chastity Theme in Comedy

In Elizabethan comedy one finds the judgment of foreign visitors about English women fully confirmed. The wives enjoy surprizing liberty, and infidelity in the husband is always justly punished in one way or another by the wife. On the whole the difficulties are settled in the interest of conventional morality. A few instances will suffice. Sir John Falstaff's intrigues in the *Merry Wives* result, as they properly should, in his discomfiture. Mistress Mayberry in *Northward Hoe* refuses to listen to the adulterous wooing of Greenfield, who to be revenged brags before her husband of having won her to his will. The slandered lady bears her Lord's anger patiently and bides her time until, at the end of the play, she discovers him in a situation innocent enough but apparently very compromising. She strikes at the right moment and they call quits. Greenfield, himself, has meantime been justly punished by the agony of a mild attack of growing horns. Mistress Open-work who figures in the sub-plot of the *Roaring Girl* knows how to deal with lusty suitors. She leads Goshawk on, makes him believe she will favor him with an assignation and then exposes him before her husband and lectures him for presuming on her modesty. The whole plot of *Westward Hoe* is built about the subject of wifely honour. Mistress Justiniano frees herself from the unwelcome suit of the Earl and calls his bawd, Mistress Birdlime,

by her true name. The second plot deals with three town's-men who
think to make a merry party with three citizen's wives at an inn in
Brainford.   But they find themselves locked out of the women's
chamber and denied the joys they had expected.   The adventure
serves to cure the three husbands, who come post-haste after their
wives, of a fondness for the society of Mistress Birdlime's lodgers.
Thus justice is evenly distributed and no harm done to morality.
Maidens figure little in comedy of this sort, for reasons already explained.   When they do appear they are a trifle hoydenish like Bess
Bridges in the *Fair Maid of the West* and Moll in the *Roaring Girl*.
But they move among seamen and roarers and tavern-brawlers without suspicion of immodesty.   Bess can don male attire and give a
beating to any man who becomes too familiar in his manners;   Moll
gives short shrift to lechers and is capable of defending chastity by
word and by deed.   Actually she was not above reproach, for she is
an historic figure, but the requirements of morality necessitated a reformation in her character before she could make a stage appearance.

VI

THE SINNERS

Innocence and patience are admirable but unexciting qualities.
The foregoing survey of Elizabethan plays extolling these virtues in
woman has not afforded consequently, except in a few instances, any
startling revelations of dramatic power nor has it revealed any significant departures from an accepted code of sexual ethics.   It should have
made clear, however, what the code is.   In the first place it is man-
devised.   Honour, the man's honour, is the important factor in it.
The glory of the chaste and patient wife consists equally in the pre-
servation of her own good name and her husband's honour.   The oper-
ation of the double standard is the more conspicious because, as I
remarked in the beginning, for the first time in the history of literature
the problems of the sex-relation receive varied and minute consideration.
The converse code forms the ethical standard in the next group of
plays to be reviewed—plays in which the sinning woman is the principal figure.   Whereas in the reconciliation dramas thus far studied
the long-suffering wife eventually brings the sinner back to the fold
and forgets the past, in the plays of the erring wife the most magnani-

mous husband kills his wife with kindness, reconciliation with her taking place only as death concludes the scene. Married love with duty for one party and obedience for the other is the ideal; declination from the ideal on the husband's part is a regrettable but not a criminal offense. True love cannot exist outside the marriage bond— at least that is the code. To see where there is conformity and where there is disagreement, which dramatists accept the received standard and which defy it, for there is naturally more frequent revolt in these plays, will be the concern of the next few pages.

The first English play of romantic love, if we except the *Interlude of Calisto* and *Melibea, Gismond of Salerne,* shows the authors struggling to correct the frank animalism of the Boccaccian original and make the story possible for an English audience which was thus far little acquainted with any heartier dramatic diet than that afforded by the moralities. I have already called attention to the strong didactic framework erected about it (Chapter II). It was obviously impossible to alter the main outline of the plot without destroying the whole story, but what could be done was done. Gismond appears in England a sorrowing widow and a dutiful daughter although Boccaccio supplies no suggestion for this conception of the heroine. But the great difference is found in the attitude of the two Gismonds toward their sin. Boccaccio's lady puts the onus on her father: he has failed to provide her with a second husband, she is a widow and having known the joys of love cannot forgo them. His objection that Guiscard is ignoble, she declares, invalidates his whole argument because it implies that a liaison with some more noble lover would not have irritated his moral sensibilities. The English heroine attempts no self-justification. She is resigned to her father's will though her feeble reply to his request for her defense, if she has one, is tearfully reproachful:

> But sithe it so hath settled in your minde,
> that neither he shall live, nor you will be
> the father, or the prince, whom we may finde
> such, as my falsed hope behight to me,
> as his deserts in service to your grace
> do justly claime, or as my ruthefull teres
> do humbly crave: if neither in this case
> for him may he, nor I appease the fearce
> and cruel rage of grefe that straines yor hart:
> alas vain is it to ask what can I say

> Why I shold live: sufficeth for my part
> to say I will not live and there to stay.[35]

The play concludes with sententious moralizing; in the Italian story the lovers' fate "is lamented but they are felt to be objects of envy as well as compassion."[36]

Although the pitiful tale of Queen Guenevere in the *Misfortunes of Arthur* is done when the first act is over, the attitude of the author, Hughes, toward the historic conception of this sinner merits attention. In the previous versions of her story she is pictured as taking refuge in the monastary *after* the first encounter between Arthur and Mordred, in which the latter is defeated. Thus Geoffrey: "Quod ut Ganhumarae . . . . annunciatum est, Confestim desperans ab Eberaco ad urbem Legionum diffiguit, atque in templo Julii martyris, inter monaches eiusdem caste vivere proposuit et vitam monachalem suscepit." Layamon follows this account. The prose *Brut* says she feared the wrath of Arthur; the alliterative *Morte Arthure* declares she fled and took the veil "alle for falsede, and fraude, and fere of hir loverde." Hughes places the escape to the monastery before the battle and motivates it not by fear but by repentance. He attempts to show Guenevere dominated by three moods. In the first her hatred for Arthur yields to a sense of shame. Fronia, her lady in waiting, is responsible for the conversion, her persuasive argument being, "A ladies best revenge is to forgive." Next the Queen appears contrite; she aphorizes over her sin, very properly blames her own fraility, and excuses the Fates. The scene terminates (1, 3) with her declaration that she is going to leave the world and find refuge in a convent. In her last appearance she tries to win Mordred to a like repentance, rebukes his shameless words and urges submission to Arthur, who, she believes, will be merciful. This is indeed a new Guenevere, already contrite before Arthur's victory and her impending punishment forces contrition.

The author of *Arden of Feversham* needed only to dramatize incident by incident the details of this famous murder case of the '50's in order to produce a perfectly constructed play with the central figure

---

[35] *Gismond of Salerne,* Cunliffe, *E.E.C.T.*, p. 198, ll. 71-82.

[36] J. W. Cunliffe, "Gismond of Salerne," *PMLA*, xxi, pp. 435-461. The pertinent passage in Boccaccio reads: Il Re con rigido visso disse, Poco prezzo mi parebbe la vita mia a dover dare per la metà diletto di quello che con Guiscardo ebbe Ghismonda.

a sinning woman. There was no necessity of pointing the moral for Justice had descended swiftly and relentlessly on the accomplices as well as the principals in the crime. In all but two important matters the author follows the record found in Holinshed. The story there tells how Mistress Arden, having yielded to the suit of Mosbie, conspires with him to accomplish her husband's murder. Their attempts fail repeatedly until at last by an elaborately worked-out scheme Arden is murdered while playing at tables in his own house. The circumstances are quickly ferreted out and punishment accorded the guilty. Mistress Arden appears in Holinshed as a bourgeoise Clytemnestra, unswerving in her determination to be rid of her husband. When convicted no prolonged lamentation escapes her lips but her penitence is sufficiently evident in the words which the historian records:

"Oh, the blood of God helpe, for this blood have I shed."

In the main this conception of her character is retained in the play but an analysis of the motive which determines her actions has been successfully attempted; the result is a delineation of character unequalled in any English drama of this kind for twenty years.[37] The author chose not to follow his source in ignoring the fact that Arden was actually a wittol, or at least winked at his wife's unfaithfulness because he feared to lose the benfit "which he hoped to gain at some of her friends' hands." Symonds maintains the loss of this element in the play weakens the dramatic structure. It would appear that the playwright omitted it in order to clarify the issue, make Arden the whiter thereby and his wife's sin the blacker. The intention seems to be to throw the whole emphasis on her guilty love, a love which amounts to an almost hypnotic fascination, as the fifth scene in the third act, for which there is no hint in Holinshed, indicates. Alice enters to Mosbie with a prayer-book in her hands. Her conscience has been at work and she has resolved to be "Arden's honest wife" henceforth. He turns upon her with a vile speech of repudiation, made the more vile through the fact that the audience knows he loves her only for his own selfish ends. Her good resolutions are beaten down at once. His power over her is too great to be resisted and she cries piteously:

Looke on me Mosby, or Ile kill my selfe.

She vows to burn her prayer-book wherein she learned her shame. She begs a look, a word. He returns with reproaches, still sullen and

[37] *Arden* was entered on the Register, April 3, 1592.

spiteful. She melts completely, as he knew she would, and he promises
to forget the quarrel. There is no avoidance of the issue. The author
meets it squarely and puts into the mouth of his sinning heroine the
only words which will quite thoroughly and convincingly explain her
guilt: [38]

> Wilt thou not looke? Is all thy love overwhelmde?
> Wilt thou not heare? What malice stopes thine ears?
> Why speaks thou not? what silence ties thy tongue?
> Thou hast bene sighted as the eagle is,
> And heard as quickly as the fearefull hare,
> And spoke as smoothly as an orator,
> When I have bid thee heare or see or speak,
> And thou art sensible in none of these?
> Waigh all thy good turns with this little fault,
> And I deserve not Mosbie's muddy lookes. (III, 5, 123-132)

Heywood, who has received certainly his meed of praise for his
handling of the problem of the sinning wife, has no such power of
character analysis in a crucial situation of this particular kind. He
slights the seduction scenes in both *A Woman Killed with Kindness*
(1603) and *Edward IV* (1594). In the first instance the beginning
gives earnest of more than the conclusion fulfills. Wendoll speaks of
love with the passionateness characteristic of all stage villains. Mistress
Frankford's answer is finely conceived:

> The host of heaven forbid
> Wendoll should hatch such a disloyal thought.

[38] The didactic element is entirely lacking in the play. The author has elaborated Alice's few words of repentance into four speeches but the situation demands
at least that. Fidelity to the bare simplicity of Holinshed's account has been
achieved although the necessary motivation has been added. It is amusing to see
how Lillo and Hoadley in their eighteenth century version of the same story revised the facts to make them acceptable to the taste of the age. Alice (now Alicia)
had been Mosby's bethrothed but cruel parents forced her to wed Arden whom she
never really loved. Her conscience troubles her throughout the play; she cannot screw up her courage sufficiently to carry through the murder of her husband. She finally throws off her guilty love and is reconciled to him. The
murder takes place without her connivance and against her will.

Another Elizabethan domestic tragedy, founded on the events surrounding a
murder committed in 1573, *A Warning for Fair Women* (printed 1599), is fully
equipped with moral exhortation, even to the extent of a framework of morality
figures which conduct and comment on the play somewhat in the fashion of a
Chorus. It seems likely that the immediate source of the play is an excessively
moral tract recounting the details of the murder and giving what purports to be the
confessions and penitent speeches of the guilty couple. It is reprinted in Richard
Simpson's *School of Shakespeare*, New York, 1878, Vol. II, pp. 221-239.

This is the trend of her argument in the next five speeches. She is Frankford's wife, her love for him is as precious as her soul's health. Wendoll urges her to a crime against *him*. She says nothing of *herself*. But the transition comes too swiftly. To Wendoll's next speech, which cunningly urges his love for Frankford, she replies:

> What shall I say?
> My soul is wandering, hath lost her way.
> Oh, Master Wendoll! Oh!

The conquest is speedily effected. There has been no demonstration of affection on her part; there is no reason to believe Wendoll is anything to her but a friend of her husband's. No occasion is provided for suspecting she had grown weary of marriage. We must suppose she is startled into acquiescence by the passionateness of Wendoll's wooing. In *Edward IV* the seduction of Jane Shore is more incoherent. There Heywood was dealing with a tradition which instead of aiding him in the conception of Jane's fall seems to have confused him. Thus More's account of her life in seeking a reason for her lapse from virtue stresses her love of finery and her indifference to her husband whom she had been forced to marry by her parents. The ballad preserved in *Percy's Reliques* records the tradition that it was Mistress Blague, Jane's friend, who persuaded her to yield to the King. The Jane of Churchyard's poem (included in the *Mirrour for Magistrates*), declares the glitter of the royal magnificence blinded her to sin. Heywood evidently tried to amalgamate these various *motiven*. The result is indecision. One motive he perhaps added himself—the compulsion exercised by Edward. In their last interview before she goes to court Jane says:

> If you inforce me, I have nought to say,
> But wish I had not lived to see this day.

Heywood's greatness lies rather in his command over the emotions of pathos and tenderness than in any power of comprehending the will-destroying growth of desire in the human heart.

The story of Mistress Frankford deserves attention here for one reason in particular. *A Woman Killed with Kindness* has been often praised as a realistic drama of contemporary life. It is in one respect, however, as romantic as any other play of Heywood's. In order to see why, one must know a little about Elizabethan methods of punishing adultery. It was not a crime although repeated attempts from the days of Henry VIII had been made to get it written into the statute books as a criminal offense. It seems that for a time in Puritan New England adultery was actually punishable by death although only a few instances of the execution of the law are recorded.[39] In Elizabeth's reign, as before and after, the problem was left to the church courts. The offended party might sue for a divorce of separation. In any case some punishment could be prescribed. The usual way of bringing the forgetful wife to her senses was to require her to do public penance in a sheet—as we find Jane Shore doing in the second part of *Edward IV*. A report of the Archdeacon's Court of Essex for 1576 shows a typical case. Margaret Orton, taken in adultery, has done penance in the parish church of Barking "before ye seconde lesson at Morninge prayer, upon Sonday the xviiith day of March 1575, and then was redd the first parte of the homilie against whoredome and adulterie, the people ther present exhorted to refraine from soche wickednes. . .she penitent for her offenses etc. . .(Dominus) pronunciavit eam esse sufficienter punitam."[40] We may well believe that this public ignominy was avoided whenever possible. Harrison in his *Description of England* speaks feelingly of the laxness with which adultery is punished:

"As in theft. . . . therefore, so in adultery and whoredom, I would wish the parties trespassing to be made bond or slaves unto those that received the injury, to sell and give where they listed or to be condemned to the galleys: for the punishment would prove more bitter to them than half-an-hours hanging[41] or than standing in a sheet, though the weather be never so cold.[42]

Another case (reported by Furnivall in his *Child Marriages, Divorces, and Ratifications*, E.E.T.S.) gives the sad story of one Elizabeth Shuttleworth which illuminates suprisingly Heywood's play. This poor wife had committed adultery with her neighbour, Peter Hartley, and born one child by him which her husband had unsuspectingly supposed the seventh of his own brood. She cannot accuse her husband of having wronged her; she swears she knew no other man besides Peter. Asked if she was allured by fair promises to confess or forced to it, she replies:

"no for she doth hit only to save her othe, and discharge her Conscience, because hit is a matter of Truthe. beynge asked howe she will lyve hereafter,

[39] A. M. Davis, *The Law of Adultery and Ignominious Punishments*, Worcester, Mass., 1895, p. 15.

[40] William Hale, *Series of Precedents of the Archdeacon's Court of Essex*, London, 1847, the 484th case.

[41] This probably refers to the custom whereby the man was required to stand in the pillory with a noose about his neck and not to any actual hanging.

[42] Camelot edition, p. 242.

sins she cannot marry, and her husband hath refused her she sais she knowis not, but as God will provide for her, beynge threatnid to do penaunce, she desires [the Chancellor] to be good to her and she will do what she shal be assigned to do." (p. 80, *op. cit.*)

Here the problem is condensed into a few lines. The sinner is refused by her husband; she cannot remarry. How will she live? As God provides. The whole matter belongs as much in the realm of economics as of ethics. Her difficulties are as much monetary as moral. Now look at the case of Mistress Frankford. Soberly considered, with this evidence in mind, the dramatic scene in which she pleads for a speedy death (IV,5) is artistic embellishment and not life.

We are made to believe Frankford does a magnanimous act in sparing her the thrust of his sword. While the audience no doubt relished this fine theatric flourish, they were sure also to appreciate the matter-of-fact kindness of his subsequent act. Instead of forcing her to do public penance and casting her aside by divorce, which would mean beggary unless kind-hearted relatives took her in, he assures her food and shelter at least, if not the restoration of his affection. His kindness does not consist in his sparing her life but rather in his continuing to shelter her from an unfeeling world after she has forfeited all right to such protection.

Commentators have justly praised the magnificent last act of the play where Heywood's peculiar talent for heart-rending pathos finds sufficient scope. The scene barely escapes being tragic and that merely because the figures are not of tragic stature. Precisely the same situation develops in Jane Shore's story—a wife who has suffered and is truly penitent, a husband who has been mercifully stern only by the restraining of his natural emotions. Heywood's conception of sin and the forgiveness of sin incarnates the Christian ideal but one cannot help observing that reconciliation in both these plays comes when the sinner is at the point of death.[48]

We have now to review four plays which have for their central figure no seduced citizen's wife, who while she wades into sin, looks back with regret to the safe ground she has left behind, but a noble

---

[48] Heywood's tendency to moralize is evident in both plays. Jane and Mistress Frankford find occasion to exhort their sisters in the audience. The latter cries out:

Oh, women, women, you that yet have kept
Your holy matrimoniall vow unstain'd,
Make me your instance; when you tread awry,
Your sinnes, like mine, will on your conscience ly. (IV, 5, 105-108)

mistress. The mood changes from *largo e teneramente* to *appassionato con brio*. Marston's *Insatiate Countess* (c. 1610) I wish to discuss first. He found the story in *Painter's Palace of Pleasure,* the tale of the Countess of Celant, which he followed in the main. Briefly the plot of the play is this. The widow Isabella at her husband's bier agrees to marry Count Roberto. On their wedding night a mad passion for the Count Massino leads her to escape to Pavy with him before the marriage is consummated. Almost immediately thereafter lust for his friend Gniaca brings her to desert Massino and deny him her chamber. He retaliates by libelling her through the city. Infuriated she persuades Gniaca to kill him, but friendship prevails over lust and the two men desert her, relieved to be emancipated from her charms. She now sells her love to Don Sago, the price being the murder of her two ex-lovers. But he is caught, confesses, and she is brought to the scaffold, still haughtily indifferent to the claims of morality. The scene at the place of execution contains the only bit of thoughtful characterization in the play. Isabella speaks ironically of Sago's "manly loyalty" and wishes him joy in both worlds, begs to be commended to the "noble Count Gniaca"—here her courage departs and she begs mercy in a broken sentence. The judge is relentless. She curses him magnificently and is about to go unrepentant to her death, dying as she had lived, a great sinner. The source, which bristles with sententious moralizing, makes her repent in the orthodox fashion and die cleansed of her faults. But Marston has another trick to turn which he may have learned from any of the reconciliation plays popular in his day. He brings in the Count Roberto, her husband, now a friar, to recall her to the path of righteousness and she makes a good end by his help. It is probably foolish to speculate why Marston chose to depart from his source at this point, for the Count of Celant in the original story, disgusted with his wanton wife, makes no attempt to win her back and in fact disappears from the tale after the Massino episode. But one inference is possible, aside from that which would assign the change to a desire to complicate the plot: convention demanded that the Countess should not die with her sins unforgiven by the man she had offended and Marston was willing to make this concession to the public demand for a moral ending.

In the absence of any definite source for Chapman's *Bussy D'Ambois* it is impossible to say precisely what the intentional alterations in the historic character of Montsurry's wife may have been. Certainly he has built up the rôle far beyond the warrant in the nearest contemporary account of Bussy's love-affair, the seventeenth story in Rosset's *Histoires Tragiques,* where under fictional names the episode is related. It is evident that he laboured over the part for, as Professor Parrott observes, touch after touch reveals his desire "to give reality to his conception" and the character does grow with consistency and fidelity to nature. Tamyra first confesses her love in a soliloquy which shows that the ties of honour and religion have been loosened. The interview with Monsieur in which she repulses him follows immediately, a wise juxtaposition of moods to indicate how unswerving is her love for Bussy. Upon that comes her husband's insistence that she bear with Monsieur's advances, a request calculated to feed with the fuel of resentment the blazing fire of her love. The lines spoken before Bussy and the Friar appear to her show her slowly sinking before what she now regards as inevitable:

> I love what most I loathe, and cannot live
> Unless I compass that which holds my death. (II, 2, 121-122)

After the rendezvous fear seizes her and conscience begins to work. She becomes cognizant of the tyranny of sin from which

> When it hath gather'd head . . . .
> No roof, no shelter can secure us . . . . (III, 1, 17-18)

When Bussy and the Friar are gone she speaks no longer of guilt or conscience but resorts to the fatalistic argument:

> What shall weak dames do, where the whole work of nature
> Hath a strong finger in each of us? (III, 1, 66-67)

The inner struggle is over. Her lord becomes physically revolting to her. She dissembles to him in an elaborate protestation of innocence (IV, 1). In the torture scene her great bodily suffering forces repentance from her, as in *The Maid's Tragedy* (1609-1610), the point of Melantius' sword directed at her life, Evadne sees her fault for the first time and confesses it. But Tamyra's love for Bussy is by no means extinct. She tries to warn him of his danger and when he dies she laments his fall. Montsurry comments on this:

> Still sitting by
> And mourning his fall more than her own fault.

But conscience eventually triumphs. In the speech beginning, "O

wretched piety that art so distract," there comes a turning and the
lines end with the distracted cry:

> Oh husband! dear friend! O my conscience.

Forgiveness follows though the sinning wife is put away, for Montsurry's honour will not suffer reconcilement. The result of this meticu-
lous care in the developing of Tamyra's rôle may not be a character
which impresses one with its spontaneity. The art may not be completely lost in the picture but Chapman at least attempted what so
talented a playwright as Heywood saw no necessity for attempting—
a complex study of a woman ruled by her passions. The sequel
to *Bussy,* the *Revenge,* reveals a very different Tamyra. Her whole
being vibrates for revenge; her penitent words are forgotten. She
directs at her cruel husband what is, as far as I can discover, the
only elaborate defense of the single standard in the Elizabethan drama:

> Though yourselves be common as the air,
> We must not take the air, we must not fit
> Our actions to our own affections;
> But as geometricians, you still say,
> Teach that no lines nor superficies
> Do move themselves, but still accompany
> The motions of their bodies; so poor wives
> Must not pursue, not have their own affections;
> But to their husbands' earnests and their jests,
> To their austerities of looks and laughters
> (Though ne'er so foolish and injurious),
> Like parasites and slaves, fit their disposures.   (I, 2, 50-61)[44]

Aside from this one scene Chapman makes little of Tamyra in the
Revenge, as indeed, there was no occasion for him to do otherwise.
The badly botched conclusion in which the cowardly Montsurry
dies with forgiveness on his lips for Tamyra and Clermont, and
the ladies exeunt to a convenient convent, is apparently a concession
to the demand that the characters should all make a good end.

At last in the *Maid's Tragedy* (1609-1610) and the *White Devil*
(1611) the theme of the sinning woman is entirely emancipated from
the bonds of conventional morality and didactic purpose with the
result that two completely rounded characters, Evadne and Vittoria,

---

[44] Professor Parrott has noted the curious fact (*The Tragedies of George Chapman,* p. 580) that these lines occur in almost identical form in Chapman's poem
A Good Woman, drawn from Plutarch's *Conjugalia Praecepta,* xii. In the poem,
however, they are used to describe the proper conduct for a wife.

emerge, each made fully expressive of the desires and gusty passions which determine her nature. The twin-dramatists have been blamed for allowing inconsistencies in the drawing of Evadne but they were constructing, one must realize, an intricate character, no simple Mistress Frankford in whom two moods only are to be discerned—joy in the love of her husband and remorse for her betrayal of that love. The very inconsistencies help to convey this sense of complexity as they have in the case of Hamlet, and the scene by scene method of construction which the authors employed is in many ways admirably fitted for their task. One gift which Beaumont and Fletcher possessed and which should be praised rather than disprized as Mr. More does, is their ability to represent life as a "tangle of passions."[45] To those who follow authoritarian ethical standards life is indeed a simple matter and dramatists who represent it in accordance with such standards find the resolution of their plots accordingly simple. But in 1610 the old standards were breaking down, particularly for the audience these authors served and they could not, if they would be faithful to life as they knew it, find easy solutions for their dramatic problems. In *A King and No King* Beaumont and Fletcher depict a phase of human life not explored previously in the drama: a mind which supposes itself proof against any turbulence finds that passion can overthrow it and leave the will, though conscious of the issue, helpless to act. In the *Maid's Tragedy* the problem is even more involved. Evadne finds she cannot wipe out her guilt in an ablution of the King's blood. She is faced with an insoluble difficulty. How may Justice be applied? What would be gained in the solution if the code of Christian ethics were applied? The only escape is a death of expiation, as tragic a death as we shall find in Elizabethan drama because it is self-inflicted by a wretched soul who can nowhere discover an answer to the riddle of her life.

When Swinburne said, "There is no poet morally nobler than Webster," he did not refer necessarily to his high indignation at injustice and his wrathful invectives against the usual sins of the world. The reasonableness of his statement can be understood by pondering the situation in the *White Devil*. Externally the play is hideous; it should revolt any sensitive person. Baldly described it is the story of a

[45] The strictures laid upon the authors by Mr. P. E. More (*Nation*, Apr. 24, 1913) are answered by Mr. Gayley in detail in his *Beaumont, the Dramatist*, p. 355-358.

lustful woman who encourages her lover to kill his wife and her
husband to make their love the safer, who defies justice with a devilish
shrewdness and who dies only faintly conscious of the upheaval in the
moral world her rioting had caused.   Where can morality be found in
such a scheme of things?   In the first place the heroine is no weak
creature, no coward before her own deeds.   She possesses the nobility
sprung from courage which Aristotle required of a tragic figure.   She
comes of the race which nourished Tamburlaine and Richard of Gloster,
Medea and Lady Macbeth.   But this would not be enough to wring
pity from us for her fall.   We no longer worship brute courage; we
demand to know what it supports and fights for.   Symonds would
see unworthy ambition, the longing to be a duchess, as the ruling
passion of Vittoria's life.   But tragedy cannot be built on that, especially when there is not present the mitigating circumstance of an
inner struggle as in *Macbeth* where ignoble ambition *is* the tragic flaw
which brings about the catastrophe.   We must seek elsewhere for
the impulse to her behaviour, and it is to be found in her love for
Brachiano.   There is abundant evidence that this love exists, in spite
of the fact that Webster's dramatic method reveals states of mind
by lightning flashes and not by soliloquies and long expository dialogue.
Flamineo's ruling passion *is* that Vittoria shall be Brachiano's duchess
and his grotesque garrulity in the matter obscures the fact that she is
only an acquiescent party to his scheming.   To interpret the quarrel-
scene between the lovers as dissembling on Vittoria's part is to
read into the lines unwarrantable innuendo.   Elizabethan dramatic
technique was primitive to the extent at least that it prepared the
audience for dissimulàtion.   Hamlet ostentatiously puts his antic disposition on; Isabella in this same play prepares to act the virago and
mystify her brother and the Cardinal.   If Webster, who next after
Jonson is the most careful of Elizabethan dramatists, had intended
this scene to be taken at other than its face value, we may be sure
he would have hinted at the desired interpretation.

Further proof of this love is provided at the death of Brachiano.
Lodovico proclaims it.   The others cry, "Rest to his soul."   Vittoria,
the only time in the play, betrays weakness.   She loses her self-control
and weeps.

> *Vittoria*   O me! this place is hell.
> *Francesco*   How heavily she takes it.
> *Flamineo*   O yes, yes
>   Had women navigable rivers in their eyes,
>   They would dispend them all—

and he continues with cynical observations about woman's tears and griefs. These few words reveal a life. Mr. Greg has interpreted the situation thus: "She sees done to death before her eyes the only man who in force of will and spirit was her equal, who was bound by community of glorious desires and unscrupulous purpose, and in whose want her life must thenceforth be void and incomplete."[46] It is the strength of her love, even an unworthy love if you will, though Cleopatra's is akin to it, which makes her a figure for a great tragedy. Two deliberate alterations of history on Webster's part tend to show that this view of the play must be something like his own. Brachiano, actually, was a gross and repulsive man, an impossible object of love for even a whited devil. If Webster had intended the motive of ambition to be considered the chief impulse in Vittoria's career, how could he have shown this better than by retaining the historic Brachiano? Camillo has, in addition, been made a moronic absurdity, deserving in any eugenic civilization little better than death. The historic Camillo (really Francesco Peretti) lived happily for a time with his wife and was by no means a model for the husband of the Vittoria of the drama.

It is surely a far cry from Wilmot's Gismond, sinful but mute and incapable of defending her sin, to Webster's Vittoria, splendidly guilty and capable of a noble rage against her enemies. In these two plays one can see how far the Elizabethan drama travelled technically and philosophically in a little more than thirty years.

The subject of the Elizabethan drama and woman is well-nigh inexhaustible. There are many more sinners whose fate it would be profitable to examine, women like Lady Macbeth for example, whose fault, unlike Vittoria's, lies not in their blood. I cannot omit, however, a word about whores and courtesans, those indispensable adjuncts to Elizabethan drama. The playwrights seldom leave them as bad as they find them. Often they find them a good husband to make them honest, if not by straightforward tactics then by trickery. Doll in *Northward Hoe* gets Featherstone; the Country Wench in *Michaelmas Term* marries, we suppose, Master Lethe. Sometimes they are sent to the House of the Convertites, like Florence in the *Fair Maid of Bristol*. Marston inflicts upon his Dutch Courtesan the "extremest whip and jail" for her offense has been notorious. Heywood does the least he may in requiring a whore (in *Royal King and Loyal Subject*) to say while reflecting upon some harsh words directed at her trade,

[46] W. W. Greg, "Webster's White Devil," *Mod. Lang. Quarterly*, Dec. 1900, p. 119.

"Such another discourse would make me goe neere to turn honest."

But I am willing to venture that there is not in all this literature such a conversion as that of Venus herself in the *Cobbler's Prophecy* (?1593). After succeeding in her plot to cuckold Mars, she is requited by her lover's desertion. She is lamenting her sad state:

> Oh that my woe would other women warne,
> To love true wedlocke or the virgin's life:
> For me too late, for them fit time to learne,
> The honour of a maid and constant wife,
> One is adorde by Gods with holy rites,
> The last like Lampes both earth and heaven lights.
> But the foule horror of a harlots name,
> Even of the Lecher counted as a scorne:
> Whose forhead beares the marke of hatefull shame,
> Of the lust-lover hated and forlorne.
> O such is Venus, so shall all such bee
> As use base lust, and foule adulterie.

JUSTICE IN ELIZABETHAN TRAGEDY

Hope teaches men to believe in the ultimate reason and justice of a moral order in the universe. Daily experience with evil in the world convinces us, however, that in this life, at least, virtue is not always triumphant. The dramatist whose concern is with the mystery of existence must adopt one of two attitudes toward this most fundamental problem: he may represent absolute justice operating with constancy in the affairs of men, which is contrary to his experience, or he may permit the innocent to suffer with the guilty, compensating for the unrelieved tragedy of such a picture by so manipulating his story that man's nobility in the face of this lawful and inexplicable fact of life will relieve the harrowed feelings of his audience. To this first conception of justice, for some unknown reason the term "poetic" has been given in spite of the fact that most of the great poets have refused to employ it.

Poetic Justice, however necessary as a theological concept, is open to grave objections as an artistic medium. In the first place it requires that men be divided into two mutually exclusive groups, the good and the bad, the sheep and the goats. It sets up in this world a kind of premature Last Judgment. It allows for no nuances of character. Whenever it is introduced as a solution for a dramatic situation tragedy becomes impossible. Aristotle declared the double conclusion with "an happy and an unhappy ending for the better and worse agents respectively" inferior and used only because audiences are not able to endure the highest tragic tension. "The pleasure arising from this double structure is not the distinctive pleasure of tragedy. It is rather one that belongs to Comedy where the deadliest of legendary foes, like Orestes and Aeggisthus, become friends, and quit the stage without anyone slaying or being slain."[1]

The Renaissance critics, as I have noted before, failed to interpret Aristotle correctly in every instance. In spite of this express statement against Poetic Justice many of them, although their commentaries purport to be inspired by his opinions found reason to favour it just

[1] Lane Cooper, *Aristotle on the Art of Poetry*, New York, 1913, p. 43.

as they develop a theory of the moral function of the drama contrary to his statement of the purpose of tragedy. In fact this feigned justice becomes an almost necessary adjunct to didacticism in the drama. Benedetto Varchi is the chief promulgator of the theory of Poetic Justice among the Italians. He holds that poetry teaches morality better than the other arts because it may instruct not by precept but by example. Its business is to remove vices from men and incite them to virtue. To him the *Divine Comedy* is a supreme work of art because in it evil men are fearfully punished and the virtuous are rewarded.[2]

Sir Philip Sidney, one scarcely needs to say, was a believer in Poetic Justice. He rates poetry above history as a teacher of men because it may picture the ideal world:

For, indeed, poetry ever setteth virtue so out in her best colors, making Fortune her well-waiting handmaid, that one must needs be enamoured of her. Well may you see Ulysses in a storm, and in other hard plights; but they are but exercises of patience and magnanimity, to make them shine the more in the near following prosperity. And, of the contrary part, if evil men come to the stage, they ever go out—as the trágedy writer answered to one that misliked the show of such persons—so manacled as they little animate folks to follow them.[3]

Although discussions of Poetic Justice appear frequently enough in English criticism of this period to make it evident that many considered it important, and while it was actually put in practise in early Elizabethan plays, it is evident that Shakespeare and his contemporaries had little use for it as a working principle. Dr. Johnson objected to *Hamlet* and *Lear* on this ground. Commenting on the latter play he says:

A play in which the wicked prosper, and the virtuous miscarry may doubtless be good, because it is a just representation of the common events of human life; but, since all reasonable beings naturally love justice, I cannot easily be persuaded that the observation of justice makes a play worse; or that, if other

[2] Varchi's position is outlined by Spingarn, *Literary Criticism in the Renaissance,* pp. 50-52.

[3] *Art of Poesy,* ed. by Cook, p. 21. Poetic Justice is implied by Puttenham in Chapter XVI of his *Art of Poesy.* Bacon says in the *Advancement of Learning:* "True history propoundeth the success and issue of actions not so agreeable to the merits of virtue and vice, therefore poesy feigns them more just in retribution *and more according to revealed providence."* (Edition of 1808, Vol. II, p. 167). Ben Jonson has been referred to as an exponent of the theory because of his statements in the dedication of *Volpone.* It is to be noticed, however, that he there declares it the office of the *comic* poet to imitate justice, thus placing himself in entire accord with Aristotle.

excellencies are equal, the audience will not always rise better pleased from the final triumph of persecuted virtue.[4]

Johnson preferred Tate's version of the Lear story—as all his contemporaries seem to have done—in which Gloster, Kent, and Lear retire to a close cell to reflect on their past life and Cordelia and Edgar become the rulers of the kingdom. His strictures on *Hamlet* hold the revenge instigated by the ghost purposeless because it is obtained by the death of "him that was required to take it." The deserved fate of Claudius is offset by the "untimely death of Ophelia, the young, the beautiful, the harmless, and the pious."[5]

The Doctor obviously mistook and was therefore entirely unsympathetic toward the Elizabethan conception of dramatic justice, for the practise of Shakespeare may rightfully be considered the norm. In his plays the doers of evil perish in accord with our hope and desire but they drag down to destruction the good that is in them or surrounds them. The moral world is not shown as consisting of two great opposed forces engaged in a war which results in the overthrow of evil but rather, as Professor Bradley analyzes it, as an organism within which a violent poison works which must be thrown off if it is to live. The struggle to rid itself of this poison of evil leaves the organism exhausted. "We remain confronted with the inexplicable fact, or the no less inexplicable appearance, of a world travailing for perfection, but bringing to birth, together with glorious good, an evil which it is able to overcome only by self-torture and self-waste. And this fact or appearance is tragedy."[6] The critic must be cautious, however, lest he read into this drama philosophy of which the playwrights had no notion. It is erroneous to believe that even the greatest of them attempted to exemplify any system of philosophy. The Elizabethan drama is seldom concerned with mental abstractions but with physical realities, emotions, passions, and the deeds they engender. We, wise after the event, observe that these pictures of life possess common elements which may be unified. But in seeking to discover such unifying factors, one must never forget that he is interpreting the dramatists who had no wish to interpret themselves. Having refused to accept the dogmatic philosophy of the earlier drama, they had no desire to be bound with a new philosophical scheme of life

[4] Criticism quoted in Variorum *Lear*, p. 419.
[5] Variorum *Hamlet*, Vol. II, p. 146.
[6] A. C. Bradley, *Shakespearean Tragedy*, London, 1924, p. 39.

of their own devising. That we may observe development with certain fairly constant elements does not mean that this evolution was a conscious matter.

The morality, as we have seen, held the English stage until the last decade of the sixteenth century. Since it was the dominant drama the manner in which it disposes of the problem of good and evil must be regarded as the current dramatic conception of the question of justice. I scarcely need to say that Poetic Justice prevails in the moralities. The miracle plays began with Chaos and ended with the Last Judgment. This final scene before the Throne of Heaven was the climax of the whole cycle, giving significance to all that had gone before and drawing men's minds from the petty considerations of this world to a contemplation of the Divine Justice which would eventually be dispensed to all humanity. The morality in its earliest form concludes in the same way. Humanum Genus in the *Castle of Perseverance* appears finally before the Judgment seat of God. To Mankind Jehovah grants mercy and invites him to sit at his right hand. He then proceeds to an account of the future great day of judgment "whanne Myhel his horn blowith at my dred dom" and the generations of men shall take their places on his right and on his left. Even after the final settlement in the moralities came to be made on earth by God's messengers and not in the Court of Heaven, the strict separation of the sheep from the goats, with reward for the one group and punishment for the other, continues. In the *Trial of Treasure*, for example, God's Visitation comes to impose His judgment. Lust is afflicted with terrible pains, Treasure is turned to dust by Time; the good character Trust is rewarded by the present of Consolation and a Crown. *Enough is as Good as a Feast* (c. 1560) concludes with the exit of Wordly Man, who has refused redemption, to Hell's torment. Rest appears to Heavenly Man as a just compensation for his righteous life:

> By God's great goodness I am sent unto thee,
> Rest is my name wherin the heavenly shal abide.

In these two moralities the judgment comes directly from God through his emissaries. The more secular moralities from which the theological element has almost entirely disappeared dispense justice with equal impartiality although the power is now exercised by an earthly magistrate. The Judge in the *Three Ladies of London* (printed 1584) orders Lucre off to Hell, and Love is sent to keep her company. In *Like*

Will to Like, the title page of which states the author's intention to
"declare" the rewards of virtue and vice, the rogues receive appropriate
sentences while Virtuous Life concludes with a short account of his
blessing in this world.

This universal custom of the judicial ending was difficult to maintain in certain of the classical stories which the early dramatists
adapted for the English stage. In *Appius and Virginia,* for instance,
it is necessary for the heroine to die but she receives a posthumous
reward for her virtue nevertheless. Fame, Memory, and Reward sing
her praise and Justice promises his help to all those that imitate her
life. Meantime the extreme punishment has been accorded the in-
triguing Vice, Haphazard, and Appius is reported to have slain himself. In the interlude, *The Historye of Horestes* (printed 1567), an
even more difficult situation develops. The hero's matricide is every-
where considered as a just and necessary action. He says of it himself:

> Who offendith ye love of god, and eke mans love with willing hart,
> Must by that love have punishment, as dutey due for his desart.
> For me therfor to punnish hear, as law of gods and man doth wil,
> Is not a crime, though that I do, as thou dost saie, my mother kil. (420-423)

This view of his act is likewise taken by his sage councillors. Consequently for him to die as a result of his righteous deed or to suffer
the torments of the furies as he does in the Aeschuylean version of
the story, would be unjust. The author therefore represents him
as living happily ever after, since there is no necessity for a reconciliation between him and the outraged spiritual powers.

Of all the pre-Shakespearean dramas in which Poetic Justice prevails Gascoigne's *Glass of Government* is the most extreme in its
insistence on the "rewardes for Vertues, as well as the punishment for
Vices." The plot is nicely contrived to arrive at the moral ending.
The two elder sons neglect instruction and exhortation and achieve
the gallows and the fornicator's carting respectively; the two younger
brothers, earnest and plodding fellows with no ears for the whisperings
of Vice, rise in this world to the most exalted positions. The Epilogus
concludes succinctly:

> You see that right, which ever more hath raigned,
> And justice both, do keepe their place still,
> To cherish good, and eke to punish ill.

Such then, was the conception of justice which obtained in Elizabethan drama until the middle eighties. It represents an attitude to-

ward life and art which the new dramatists discarded just as they refused, in the main, to accept the narrowing doctrine of the didactic function of the drama. Precisely how the transformation was made and what elements determined the ultimate Elizabethan conception must now be considered.[7]

In order that the change could come about, two fundamental alterations were necessary. Somehow the notion of an ever-active, externally applied justice having its source in the Courts of Heaven and executed by heavenly ministers or God's earthly representatives must be discarded. In the second place the dualistic conception of the moral order must be replaced by some idea which would take account of the good in the worst of men and the bad in good men, and demonstrate that evil and good may exist in the same person or at least that sinners may possess qualities of greatness. To the influence of Seneca the first transformation may be ascribed; to Marlowe belongs the credit of having put on the stage characters which, though essentially evil and therefore deserving punishment, are at the same time so interesting and in one case so appealing that the audience is willing for a time to suspend judgment upon them. His contribution is a necessary step in the development of the tragedy of character.

The various effects of the impact of Seneca on the Elizabethan drama have been carefully studied. The actual verbal borrowings have been collected, the result of the imitation of his five-act form, his fondness for long description and rhetorical moralizing discussed. Due prominence has been given the fact that the revenge play with

---

[7] The settlement by supernatural agents is exemplified in a few later Elizabethan plays. Most impressive of these is Barnes' *The Devil's Charter*. Pope Alexander sells his soul to the Devil who returns to claim it when the term is up. The theme gives opportunity for a varied spectacle of extravagant and horrific crime. The epilogue concludes:

> Th' omnipotent great guider of all powers,
> (Whose essence is pure grace, and heavenly love,
> As he with glorie crownes heroyick actions,
> Bearing a taste of his eternall vertue)
> So semblably doth he with terror strike,
> In heavie vengeance sinnes detestable:
> As in this tragicke myrrour to your eyes.

Dekker's *If it be not a Good Play, the Devil is in it* shows the servants of Pluto interfering to their eventual discomfiture in the affairs of men. Dekker and Massinger in the *Virgin Martyr* suggest the continuous control of Heaven through the symbolic figures of Harpax and Angelo.

its important instrument, the vindictive ghost, originates with Seneca
—at least as far as Elizabethan origins are concerned. The horrors
of Seneca, the bloody banquet, the poisonings, the brutal maimings
and murders, were relished by the English of the Renaissance, an
age which had for its shibboleth, "Everything in excess." But Seneca's
most important lesson for the dramatists was to show them how to
search in the hearts of their characters for the source of their actions.
This may seem like an extravagant statement in view of the heavy
pall of fatalism which appears to hang over his plays. But this fatalism
is external and inorganic and receives scant recognition in the conclusions of the dramas. In the Greek plays which Seneca imitated, the
gods have much to do in settling the issue of the tragic struggle.
Seneca, however, never introduces a god or goddess actively interfering
in person with human destiny. Juno, it is true, declares her intention
in the *Hercules Furens* of punishing Hercules for his Jovinian origin
but her opening soliloquy constitutes her only appearance. In Euripides her messengers come to earth to drive him to madness. In the
Senecan *Phaedra* the part of divinity in shaping the ends of the play
is negligible whereas in the *Hippolytus* of Euripides Diana appears
to Theseus and reveals to him directly the truth about Phaedra's
infatuation and in the end Hippolytus is reconciled to the goddess.
The situation in the *Thyestes* has a direct bearing on the evolution
of Elizabethan dramatic justice. The Fury and the Ghost of Tanta-
lus appear as prologue. The Fury tries to compel the Ghost to inspire
revenge in the heart of the earthly representatives of his family, and
when it refuses, forces willingness from it by a threatened scourging.
But the Ghost does not enter again to communicate with Atreus.
We are perhaps supposed to believe it breathes into his heart the spirit
of revenge. In the second act Atreus feels the fury rising in him:

> Some greater evil lurks within my soul,
> And monstrous, swells beyond all human bounds,
> My sluggish hands impelling to the deed.
> I know not what it is; but this I know
> That 'tis some monstrous deed.[8]

Justice in the *Thyestes*, though demanded by an ocult being, is exacted
by a human agent. It is precisely this conception that is embodied
in *The Spanish Tragedy* and *Locrine*. The significance of the change
must not be overlooked. In the Greek drama, and in a crude fashion

---

[8] P. 301 in the translation of F. J. Miller, Chicago, 1907.

in the moralities as well, divinity is shown directly concerned and actively engaged in human affairs. In Seneca and his Elizabethan imitators the executor of justice is man himself. The function of divinity is reduced to daemonic inspiration or prophecy.

The revenge motive in tragedy, based on the right and necessity of private vengeance, was particularly congenial to the Elizabethans because they could easily comprehend it. This is not to say that the vendetta flourished in England as it did in other parts of Europe. But in those turbulent times when no courtier was safe from the murderous disfavour of his sovereign, when traitors and supposed traitors were subjected to the cruellest torments, when free-thinkers were certain of the stake and Jesuits of the gallows, no man's life was worth a fig unless he was ready to defend it. Personal honour was "tickle o' the sear" and even the efforts of a great official like Bacon failed to stamp out the vice of duelling. An injury required exact payment in kind. The law allowed an unfortunate victim of the crime of mayhem to receive satisfaction by the infliction of a similar wound on the man who had attacked him. Stephen says: "The extraordinary lenity of the English criminal law towards the most atrocious acts of personal violence forms a remarkable contrast to its extraordinary severity with regard to offences against property."[9] The truth of this statement is evident from the number of instances recorded in which the wronged party acts in his own behalf. Lord Herbert's father after escaping a vicious and cowardly attack by ruffians hired by a personal enemy attempted to exact a private vengeance. Lord Herbert, himself, was restrained from doing the same after a murderous assault by Sir John Ayres only by the intervention of the Council. The Elizabethan letter-writer Chamberlain devotes the whole of a longish letter to an accurate report of an attempt on the life of Sir Charles Cavendish instigated by John Stanhope with the aid of twenty hired bravi.[10] Although it is plain that revenge for injured honour was exacted by gentlemen who felt they had been slighted or abused, it is by no means certain that the English still practised blood revenge for the murder of a friend or relative. Cases of it have found their

[9] Sir James Fitzjames Stephen, *A History of the Criminal Law of England,* London, 1883, Vol. III, p. 109.

[10] *Chamberlain's Letters,* The Camden Society, Vol. 79, no. XXI.

way into the earlier pages of Holinshed but Elizabethan records so far as I have examined them are silent.[11]

That the idea was in force on the continent there is abundant evidence. An illuminating instance of revenge for murder occured in Paris in 1583. Fourteen years previously one Sieur de Maurevert, failing to assassinate Admiral Coligny, for whose death a large reward had been offered, killed instead, as the next best venture, his lieutenant, M. de Mouy. In 1583 de Mouy's son learning that Maurevert, who had now gained the name of the "King's Killer," was in Paris, met the murderer of his father on the streets of the city and wounded him mortally. Five men were killed in the fray. The Queen proposed to have de Mouy punished but "almost all [of the Council] opposed this and represented that two great mischiefs would result: one, that gentlemen would be discouraged in their filial duty to avenge their fathers, and that the door would be open to all traitors who wished to assassinate boldly and without fear of revenge."[12] The annals of the Italian Renaissance are full of such instances. A most striking example which occurs in Benvenuto Cellini's *Autobiography* shows the impulse behind the revenge for murder, the spirit of the time which impelled the avenger to undertake his task. Benvenuto's brother had been killed by a policeman in a brawl in which he had no business to be engaged. But the deplorable affair stirred Benvenuto so deeply that he was unable to work for brooding on it. "I. . .took to watching the arquebusier who shot my brother," he writes, "as though he had been a girl I was in love with. . . . When I saw that the fever caused by always seeing him about was depriving me of sleep and appetite, and was bringing me by degrees to sorry plight, I overcame my repugnance to so low and not quite praiseworthy an enterprise, and made my mind up one evening to rid myself of the torment."[13] When he had dis-

---

[11] Sir John Holland, for example, in 1385, killed Lord Stafford whose man had shot his favorite servant. The Earl of Stafford's wisdom and patience in leaving to the King the settlement is commented upon. *Holinshed*, Vol. II, p. 766, edition of 1808.

[12] I am indebted to Dr. Paul Van Dyke for calling my attention to this case. The story is given in his *Catherine de Médicis*, New York, 1922, Vol. II, pp. 25 and 297. The quotation above is from the latter page.

[13] *Life of Benvenuto Cellini,* translated by John Addington Symonds, New York, 1906, Vol. I, pp. 217-218. The whole story of the fray and the revenge is given pp. 209-220.

patched the crossbowman with a dagger-thrust—it must be noticed that the *murder* was not the unpraiseworthy enterprise but the way in which it had to be done—he went back to work on the Pope's jewel with a relieved mind. His Holiness gave him a menacing glance at the next audience but later looked him straight in the face and said, "Now that you are cured, Benvenuto, take heed how you live." Men of the Renaissance who knew what it was to feel this desire for vengeance wrankling in their bosom could appreciate to the full the torments in the breast of Atreus or any of his literary descendants and recognize as authentic these longings for direct and personally inflicted justice. As Mr. Einstein puts it: "Perhaps one reason why the Elizabethan drama save in the greater Shakespearean masterpieces remains so dead to us, is the lack of contact between modern life and private vengeance. The Englishman of the sixteenth century had still enough associations with former recollection of violence to make the crimes of Italy appear not altogether remote."[14]

The *Spanish Tragedy* for several reasons deserves consideration in connexion with the general problem of justice in the Elizabethan drama. In the first place it is the progenitor of the most popular type of tragic-melodrama of the period, a type in which justice falls upon the evil-doer directly, swiftly and by human agency. Although the Heavens and the Furies are constantly called upon by Hieronimo to punish the guilty, this barrage of words conceals an extremely realistic action in which supernatural powers have little to do. The Ghost of Andrea and Revenge serve as prologue and chorus to expose the previous action and comment on the progress of the revenge. The Ghost groans for satisfaction and Revenge reiterates the promise that it shall be satisfied but there is no direct communication between these two extraneous figures and the human actors in the tragedy. The spirit of revenge works in Hieronimo as it does in Atreus or Benvenuto Cellini for that matter. It seems almost to be spontaneously generated. In later revenge plays the ghost assumes a major rôle, as in *Hamlet* for instance, or better still in *Antonio's Revenge* where it directs the details of the schemes evolved by the hero to avenge his father's murder. Here, however, the ghost is merely an interested spectator.

[14] Lewis Einstein, *Tudor Ideals,* New York, 1921, p. 123. It is significant that the scene of none of the revenge plays is laid in England. Italy naturally most often furnishes the background but Germany, France, and Denmark are represented. Apparently, the theme was always regarded as sufficiently remote from English life to require a foreign setting.

The fact that Hieronimo considers other solutions of his difficulties than personal revenge has not been sufficiently noted. He contemplates leaving the matter to heaven and even attempts to move the King to act in his behalf. This would seem to indicate that the author felt the necessity of justifying the actions of his hero by indicating the impossibility of trusting to either solution. He enters, III, 13, with a book in his hand and begins his soliloquy:

> Vindicta mihi![15]
> I, heaven will be revenged of every ill;
> Nor will they suffer murder unrepaide,
> Then stay, Hieronimo, attend their will:
> For mortal men may not appoint their time!

But his eye lights on the sentence: "Per scelus semper tutum est sceleribus iter," and thoughts of patience are dispelled:

> Strike, and strike home, where wrong is offered thee;
> For evils unto ills conductors be,
> And death's the worst of resolution.

He has already made an attempt to compel justice from the man who is supposed to guarantee it, the King, but the villian Lorenzo has foiled him there. In the previous scene he presses forward into the presence crying, "Justice, O justice to Hieronimo." The King's "Who is he that interrupts our business?" quells him until the mention of Horatio's name leads him to plead again:

> *Hier.* Justice, O justice, justice, gentle king.
> *King.* Who is that? Hieronimo?
> *Hier.* Justice, O, justice, O my sonne, my sonne,
> My Sonne, whom naught can ransom or redeeme,
> *Lor.* Hieronimo, you are not well-advisde.
> *Hier.* Away, Lorenzo, hinder me no more;
> For thou hast made me bankrupt of my blisse,
> Give me my sonne; You shall not ransom him! (63-70)

His mad raving puzzles the King but he makes no inquiry into its cause. Castile later refers to his strange action in quizzing Lorenzo about certain vicious rumors which are whispered at court:

> *Castile.* My selfe have seene thee busie to keepe back
> Him and his supplications from the King (III, 14, 77-78)

Thus thwarted in his attempt to obtain justice from its lawful purveyors Hieronimo receives justification for his act of vengeance.

[15] This is an interesting Christian coloring in a play which is consistently pagan in tone.

This is an element that disappears in later plays. Indeed, as the type grew in favour, the act of revenge needed less and less justification until a *reductio ad absurdum* occurs in the *Tragedy of Hoffman* (c. 1602) and the *Revenger's Tragedy* (1607) where the avengers are no better than the sinners whom they oppose. In *Hamlet* and *Antonio's Revenge* the activity of the ghost adds a kind of fatalism to the play which relieves the barbaric nature of the plot and sanctifies the act of justice.

The ethics of the revenge play did not go unrebuked. Tourneur's *Atheist's Tragedy* tries to impose on the type the theological concept, "Mihi vindicta, ego retribuam." The ghost of Montferrers appears to his son, not to urge him to revenge as the paternal ghosts were wont to do, but rather to restrain him from it:

> Return to France, for thy old father's dead,
> And thou by murder disinherited.
> Attend with patience the success of things,
> But leave revenge unto the King of kings[16]

When he arrives in France to find corroborated this terrifying report of his father's death, his sweetheart married to another, and his estate expropriated, Charlemont resolves on vengeance. But again the ghost forbids it:

> Hold, Charlemont,
> Let him revenge my murder and thy wrongs
> To whom the justice of revenge belongs[17]

In the end the soul of D'Amville, the Atheist, who has been the author of all these woes, is so preyed upon by conscience that he abjures his wickedness and kills himself with the weapon he had intended to use upon his unfortunate victim, Charlemont. Charlemont, who has obeyed the ghost's behest utters what may be regarded as the author's intended comment on the convention of revenge:

> Only to Heaven I attribute the work,
> Whose gracious motives made me still forbear
> To be my own revenger. Now I see
> That patience is the honest man's revenge[18]

When Chapman came to write his *Revenge of Bussy D'Ambois* he had

---

[16] *The Plays of Webster and Tourneur,* Mermaid Series, p. 286.
[17] *Ibid.,* p. 294.
[18] *Ibid.,* p. 336.

no mind to imitate the established type. His revenger, Clermont, is
no ordinary instrument of justice. From the first he is pictured as,

> . . . . loathing any way to give in act,
> But in the noblest and most manly course.

Revenge in other plays had been accomplished violently, in the "Italian
manner" by attack from the rear or under cover of disguise. Clermont
sends a challenge which sets the murderer Montsurry in a cowardly
tremor. When the revenge is complete and Montsurry, having for-
given Tamyra and Clermont, is about to die, he dismisses him from
this world with the words:

> Rest, worthy soul; and with it the dear spirit
> Of my lov'd brother-rest in endless peace!
> Soft lie thy bones, Heaven be your soul's abode,
> And to your ashes be the earth no load[19]

These two plays are obvious attempts to lift and refine the type. The
usual revenge play showed retribution following close on the act of
evil and imposed by a human agent animated either by the spontaneously generated spirit of revenge or the injunction of a ghostly visitor.
It also showed the innocent perishing with the guilty and frequently
the blood-guiltiness demanding death which taints even those whose
act of revenge is a duty righteously executed.

But Elizabethan tragedy by no means consists solely of plays in
which justice, executed by a human avenger, descends on a murderer.
A number of dramas exist in which the tragedy follows as a direct
result of the protagonist's peculiar defect of character. That defect
may be of a criminal nature like Macbeth's or Barabas' or it may
consist merely in a fatal indifference to the social code as in the case
of Antony or the Duke of Byron. In any event we understand that
the hero, no matter how admirable in other respects, cannot survive
if society is to continue its orderly functioning. Marlowe was the first
to exploit this kind of drama. His Tamburlaine does not fall because
what we might suppose his tragic flaw, his cruelty, is really, I think,
his chief claim to the title of the "Scourge of God." He *is* justice.
Faustus follows the theological tradition which is continued in the
Devil's Charter, and is therefore not a useful illustration. But the
Jew of Malta is an excellent example of the tragedy of character in
which the protagonist is eventually caught in the web of his own
devising or, to state it more generally, in which the erroneous or wicked

[19] V, 5, 116-119

acts for which he is responsible and their consequences become the inseparable parts of his tragedy.

In a sense, of course, the *Jew of Malta* is not a tragedy at all for tragedy implies a loss to the world of life which is potentially or actually valuable to it. The Jew who perishes in the final catastrophe is no loss to human society though he succeeds in the first two acts in arousing our admiration if not our sympathy. But this fact in no way affects the cause or nature of his fall. Barabas is a Machiavellian and the essence of Machiavellianism is astuteness. The successful prince works out his schemes alone. All his actions are dictated by policy. He is cruel, perjurious, hypocritical, vindictive, disloyal when his reason dictates the wisdom of such villainy. Marlowe places in the mouth of his prologue, Machevil himself, the essence of the princely *Staatswissenschaft:* "(I) hold there is no sinne but Ignorance."

Barabas' special cunning reveals itself in his ability to play off one party against another for their mutual destruction, a trait ultimately derived from Machiavelli's dictum that a prince should encourage and profit from the dissentions among his subjects. It is by this means that he accomplishes the deaths of Mathias and Lodowick, the suitors to his daughter. He deceives each with the promise of her hand and at the same time arouses the jealousy of each against the other. A false challenge sent by him to Mathias, purporting to be from Lodowick, results in the slaughter of the two suitors. In somewhat similar fashion he procures the deaths of the two friars, Bernardine and Jacomo. To each he makes a profession of friendship and an hypocritical confession of his sins. He encourages each to hope for the bestowal of wealth on the house he represents. With the help of his henchman Ithimore, he murders Bernardine. When Jacomo, returning, strikes the corpse which has been propped up against the doorsill, Barabas makes use of the chance accident to accuse him of murder and have him punished by the law for his own deed. Again his cunning aids him so to contrive his plots that one of his victims works his own destruction.

But his last great *coup,* which he intends shall be his crowning achievement in strategy, brings about his own fall. He meets at last with one who understands his nefariousness and excells him in cunning. The catastrophe is a beautiful example of ironic justice. Barabas, literally thrown out of the city by the Maltese, assists the Turks in their triumphant siege and is rewarded for his services by being made governor of the captured city. He shrewdly concludes that his position will be impossible to maintain unless he secures it by some politic move and so he attempts double-dealing once more. Here he makes his great error in judgment. Previously he had known only success in his favorite device of dissembling with two parties. Never for a moment does he suspect that anyone is capable of serving him in kind. Like Iago he counts on the stupidity of mankind and goes down as a result of his own myopic policy. The play has been justly criticized for the falling off in poetic brilliance and the degeneration in the character of the hero in the last three acts but Marlowe's judgment in connecting Barabas' fate with the one talent on which he most prides himself deserves high praise. Barabas is guilty of the only sin which exists in his moral code, ignorance, and he perishes as a result. Responsibilty for his ghastly end is ascribed to heaven by the Governor:

> So march away, and let due praise be given
> Neither to Fate nor Fortune, but to Heaven.

But this idea receives no stress and serves merely to provide a tag to close the play. The judgment may accord with the popular ideas of divine justice working in the world but Marlowe is at no pains to make it appear extra-mundane and providential.

In the tragedies of character which were written in later years, whether the hero is a nobleman or a villain, the circumstances of his fall are so contrived that we feel they are inseparably bound up with his perverse or criminal actions. The effect is that of a moral order in which retribution follows as a natural consequence of such actions. In the fifth act of the *Tragedy of Byron* Epernon summarizes in a speech the character of the hero of this kind of tragedy:

> Oh of what contraries consists a man!
> Of what impossible mixtures! Vice and virtue,
> Corruption, and eternesse, at one time,
> And in one subject, let together, loose!
> We have not any strength but weakens us,
> No greatness but doth crush us into air. (V, 3, 189-194)

Byron, himself, though in him the fault is less than the merit, is compounded of these elements of strength and weakness. He possesses *virtu*, which the Renaissance required of great men, but mingled with it is the overweening sense of his own indispensableness to society which leads him to believe his every act is justified *sui generis*. But the theme of his fall is not developed, as the Greeks might have treated

it, into a Nemesis drama.   There is talk of justice; Byron threatens
the Chancellor with retribution hereafter; the King reiterates the just-
ness of his cause.   But the punishment is not dictated by heaven.   The
Chancellor recognizes in Byron "a mighty merit and a monstrous
crime."   With the latter allowed to go unpunished "the King can
have no refuge for his life."   Byron's death comes then as the natural
and inevitable consequence of his failure to bend his will—a fact he
himself recognizes:

for one fault
I forfeit all the fashion of a man.

One might suppose Henry would view his act of justice as inspired by
Heaven but such is not his attitude.   He talks of the divine right of
kings but it is to be noticed that his course of action has been determined before he calls the Deity to his side of the struggle.   With *Byron*
as in the *Jew of Malta* although Heaven's interest in human affairs
receives a conventional mention the fall of the hero seems to be regarded
rather as a phenomenon than a recognizable act of Providence.   The
dramatist approaches his conclusion not to prove but to record.

And this, I think, will be found true of Shakespeare's tragedies of
character.   The supernatural plays a part in some of them.   In fact
it is largely through the use of ghosts and apparitions that he conveys
a sense of the mysteriousness of the "life in death" which is our
earthly existence.   But these creatures hover near the bourne of life.
They do not come from the throne of God laden with imprecation
or blessing.   The deaths which conclude the tragedies in which they
appear are brought about by natural causes.   All that they can do
is to "enunciate a wish or cast a flashlight into the future."[20]   Their
purpose of visitation is personal.   Even in the most fatalistic of the
dramas, *Macbeth,* where the supernatural might seem to be the controlling factor in the hero's tragedy, Shakespeare makes it quite clear
that he is a free agent and that his fate follows as a natural consequence of his failure to choose the better course.   A splendid ironic
justice is visited upon him in the fact that he deliberately chooses to
interpret the equivocations of the evil spirits as his own criminal ambition prompts.   That was his error and his undoing.

One would be bold to conjecture Shakespeare's theology but it is
evident that he had no desire to point to the fall of his heroes as a

[20] J. S. P. R. Gibson, *Shakespeare's Use of the Supernatural,* Cambridge, 1908,
p. 115.

judgment sent by Heaven. With the exception of *Richard III* the concluding lines of the tragedies have little to say of heavenly powers. Richmond, it is true, feels himself the appointed servant of God's justice. Macduff, however, whose position is comparable to Richmond's, does not identify his cause with Heaven's. Whether this lack of supernaturalism implies a conscious change of attitude on Shakespeare's part we may not say, but the fact remains that the later plays are free from the supernaturalism which characterizes *Richard III*.

This lack of supernaturalism can be demonstrated of other dramatists contemporary with him. Beaumont and Fletcher make Lysippus conclude the *Maid's Tragedy* with the couplet:

> . . . . for on lustful kings
> Unlook'd-for sudden deaths from Heaven are sent;
> But cursed is he that is their instrument.

Otherwise there is a slight reference to justice in the play. Even the death of Evadne passes without comment. Webster puts into Vittoria's mouth the only words spoken in regard to the justice of her fall:

> O, my greatest sin lay in my blood!
> Now my blood pays for't"[21]

It is odd that in the tragedies of character from Marlowe to Webster divine justice plays so slight a part. During these years with the growth of the Puritan party the doctrine of Predestination was spreading, a theology which taught heaven's direct supervision of human affairs and the close relationship between the acts of man and the decrees of God. Yet the drama moves in the opposite direction. The sinners are condignly punished still but the judgment is not administered; it grows out of the deeds of evil as a fatal flowering. Ferdinand in the *Duchess of Malfi* summarizes in three lines this kind of tragedy:

> My sister, O my sister; there's the cause on't
> Whether we fall by ambition, blood, or, lust,
> Like diamonds we are cut with our own dust.[22]

Is it possible to find a common element in these two types of Elizabethan tragedy, a trait which may be called genuinely Elizabethan? Certainly in both the debacle is excessively wasteful of human life. This wastefulness which is doubtless at basis a response to the Elizabethan love of gory spectacle whether on Tower Hill, the arena of Paris

[21] Mermaid Edition, p. 122.
[22] *Ibid.,* p. 239.

Garden or the public stage, is elevated by the great men into tragedy. If the drama refused to accept the Poetic Justice of the moralities, it gave compensation by picturing superabundantly the malignancy of evil.

BIBLIOGRAPHY

It has been my purpose to record in the foot-notes those works which I have consulted for particular points in connexion with my thesis. Consequently I have listed here only such books and monographs as have been of general recurrent use to me. It has not seemed necessary to include a detailed bibliography of the standard works without which a thesis in this field. cannot be written: the vol. umes on the drama in the *Cambridge History of English Literature* (V and VI) Chambers' *Medieval Stage* and *Elizabethan Stage,* and the histories of Fleay, Schelling, and Ward.

Boyer, Clarence. The Villain as Hero in Elizabethan Tragedy. New York, 1914.

Bradley, A. C. Shakespearean Tragedy. London, 1924.

Brooke, C. F. T. The Tudor Drama. Boston, 1911.

Brown, John. The English Puritans. Cambridge (England), 1910.

Butcher, S. H. Aristotle's Theory of Poetry and Fine Art. London, 1902.

Einstein, L. D. Tudor Ideals. New York, 1921.

Gildersleeve, V. C. Government Regulation of the Elizabethan Drama. New York, 1908.

Greg, W. W., ed. Henslowe's Diary. 2 vols. London, 1904.

Grosart, A. B., ed. The Non-Dramatic Works of Thomas Dekker. 5 vols. London, 1885.

Grosart, A. B., ed. The Life and Complete Works of Robert Greene. 15 vols. London, 1881-1886.

Grosart, A. B., ed. The Works of Thomas Nashe. 6 vols. London, 1881.

Herford, C. H. and Simpson, Percy. Ben Jonson. 2 vols. Oxford, 1925.

Heywood, Thomas. Apology for Actors. Publications of the Shakespeare Society, vol. 3. London, 1841.

Innes, Arthur. England under the Tudors. New York, 1911.

de Julleville, Petit. La comédie et les moeurs en France au moyen âge. Paris, 1886.

Klein, David. Literary Criticism from the Elizabethan Dramatists. New York, 1910.

Mackenzie, W. R. The English Moralities. Boston, 1914.

Mortensen, Johan. Le théâtre français au moyen âge. Paris, 1903.

Onions, C. T., ed. Shakespeare's England. 2 vols. Oxford, 1916.

Painter, William. The Palace of Pleasure. 2 vols. London, 1813.

Sidney, Sir Philip. The Defense of Poesy, ed. A. S. Cook. Boston, 1890.

Sisson, Charles. Le gout public et le théâtre Elisabethain. Dijon, 1921.

Spens, Janet. Elizabethan Drama. London, 1922.

Spingarn, J. E. A History of Literary Criticism in the Renaissance. New York, 1899.

Symmes, Harold. Le débuts de la critique dramatique en Angleterre jusqu' à le mort de Shakespeare. Paris, 1903.

Symonds, J. A. Shakespeare's Predecessors in the Elizabethan Drama. London, 1884.

Thompson, E. N. S. The Controversy between the Puritans and the Stage. New Haven, 1903.

COLLECTED EDITIONS OF PLAYS

With a few exceptions the plays referred to in the text, whose authors have attained the dignity of a collected edition, will be found in the following volumes.

Boas, F. S., ed. The Works of Thomas Kyd. Oxford, 1901.

Bond, R. W., ed. The Works of John Lyly. 3 vols. Oxford, 1902.

Bullen, A. H., gen. ed. Variorum Edition of the Works of Beaumont and Fletcher. 4 vols. London, 1904.

Bullen, A. H., ed. The Works of John Marston. 3 vols. Boston, 1887.

Bullen, A. H., ed. The Works of George Peele. 2 vols. Boston, 1888.

Brooke, C. F. T., ed. The Works of Marlowe. Oxford, 1910.

Collins, J. C., ed. The Plays and Poems of Robert Greene. 2 vols. Oxford, 1905.

Craig, W. J., ed. The Complete Works of William Shakespeare. Oxford, 1905.

Cunliffe, J. W., ed. The Complete Works of George Gascoigne. 2 vols. Cambridge (England), 1907-1910.·

Cunningham, Francis, ed. The Works of Ben Jonson. 3 vols. London, 1897.

Grosart, A. B., ed. The Works of Samuel Daniel. 5 vols. London, 1885-1896.

Grosart, A. B., ed. The Works in Verse and Prose of Fulke Greville. 4 vols. Fuller Worthies Library, 1870.

Hazlitt, ·W. C., ed. Webster's Dramatic Works. 4 vols. London, 1857.

Miller, F. J., trans. The Tragedies of Seneca translated into English Verse. Chicago, 1902.

Parrott, T. M., ed. The Comedies and Tragedies of George Chapman. 2 vols. London, 1910.

Pearson, John, pub. The Dramatic Works of Thomas Dekker. 4 vols. London, 1873.

Pearson, John, pub. The Dramatic Works of Thomas Heywood. 6 vols. London, 1884.

Kastner, L. E. and Charlton, H. B., eds. The Poetical Works of Sir William Alexander. 2 vols. Edinburgh, 1921.

The following general collections have furnished a number of plays:

Bang, W., gen. ed. Materialen zur Kunde des älteren Englischen Dramas. 42 vols. Louvain, 1902-1914.

Brooke, C. F. T., ed. The Shakespeare Apocrypha. Oxford, 1908.

Bullen, A. H., ed. Old Plays. 4 vols. London, 1885.

Cunliffe, J. W., ed. Early English Classical Tragedies. Oxford, 1912.

Farmer, John, ed. The Tudor Facsimile Texts.

Greg, W. W., gen. ed. The Malone Society Reprints. London, 1907——.

Hazlitt, W. C., ed. A Select Collection of Old English Plays (Hazlitt's Dodsley). 15 vols. London, 1874.

SPECIAL EDITIONS

(I have included here plays referred to in the text which are not collected in the author's editions cited above and a few special editions of plays which are collected in those editions.)

All for Money. T. Lupton. Jahrbuch der deutschen Shakespeare Gesellschaft. Vol. XL.

Appius and Virginia. "R.B." Hazlitt's Dodsley. Vol. IV.

Arden of Feversham. *** Shakespeare Apocrypha.

Birth of Merlin. *** Shakespeare Apocrypha.

Calisto and Melibea. *** Malone Society Reprints.

Cambises. Thomas Preston. Hazlitt's Dodsley. Vol. IV.

Castle of Perseverance. *** Early English Texts Society, extra series. 1904.

Christian Turned Turk. Robert Dayborne. Anglia. Vol. XX.

Cobbler's Prophecy. Robert Wilson. Malone Society Reprints.

Conflict of Conscience. Nathaniel Woodes. Hazlitt's Dodsley. Vol. VI.

Death of Robert Earl of Huntington. Anthony Munday. ed. J. P. Collier, London, 1828.

Devil's Charter. Barnaby Barnes. Bang's Materialen. Vol. VI.

Edward III. *** Shakespeare Apocrypha.

Enough is as Good as a Feast. W. Wager. Huntington Library Reprints, No. 11.

Fair Maid of Bristol. *** ed. A. H. Quinn. Univ. of Penn. Studies in Philol. and Lit. Vol. VIII.

Fleire. Edward Sharpham. Bang's Materialen. Vol. XXXVI.

Gismond of Salerne. R. Wilmot and others. Cunliffe's Early English Classical Tragedies.

Glass of Government. George Gascoigne. Works, ed. by J. W. Cunliffe.

Gorboduc. Edward Sackville and Thomas Norton. Cunliffe's E.E.C.T.

Honest Whore. Thomas Dekker. Mermaid edition, ed. Ernest Rhys.

Hoffman. Henry Chettle. ed. by Richard Ackermann, Bamberg, 1894.

Horestes. John Pickering. Quellen des weltlichen Dramas in England vor Shakespeare. Strassburg, 1898.

How a Man May Choose a Good Wife from a Bad. *** Bang's Materialen. Vol. XXXV.

Isle of Gulls. John Day. Works of Day, ed. A. H. Bullen. London, 1881.

Jocasta. George Gascoigne. Cunliffe's E.E.C.T.; also in his *Belles Lettres* edition of The Supposes and Jocasta.

Knack to Know a Knave. *** Tudor Facsimile Texts.

Larum for London. *** Malone Society Reprints.

Liberality and Prodigality. *** Malone Society Reprints.

Life and Repentance of Mary Magdelene. L. Wager. ed. by F. I. Carpenter. Univ. of Chicago Press, 1902.

Like Will to Like. Ulpian Fulwel, Hazlitt's Dodsley. Vol. III.

London Prodigal. *** Shakespeare Apocrypha.

Longer Thou Livest the More Fool Thou Art. W. Wager. Tudor Facsimile Texts.

Lust's Dominion. *** Hazlitt's Dodsley. Vol. XIV.

Miseries of Enforced Marriage. George Wilkins. Hazlitt's Dodsley. Vol. IX.

Misfortunes of Arthur. Thomas Hughes. Cunliffe's E.E.C.T.

Patient and Meek Grissill. John Phillips. Malone Society Reprints.

Patient Grissill. Thomas Dekker, Henry Chettle, William Haughton. ed. G. Hübsch. Erlanger Beiträge. Vol. XV.

Ralph Roister Doister. Nicholas Udall. ed. W. H. Williams and P. A. Robin. London, 1901. (The Temple Dramatists.)

Revenger's Tragedy. Cyril Tourneur. Mermaid edition, ed. by J. A. Symonds.

Royal King and Loyal Subject. Thomas Heywood. ed. by Kate W. Tibbals. Univ. of Penn. Studies in Phil. and Lit. 1905.

Satiromastix. Thomas Dekker. J. H. Penniman. Boston, 1913. (Belles Lettres.)

Shoemaker a Gentleman. William Rowley. Works, ed. by C. W. Stork. Univ. of Penn. Studies in Phil. and Lit. Vol. XIII.

Shoemaker's Holiday. Thomas Dekker. Mermaid edition. ed. by Ernest Rhys.

Sir Clyomon and Sir Clamydes. *** Malone Society Reprints.

Ten Tragedies. Seneca. Thomas Newton's Collection reprinted in the Publications of the Spenser Society. Nos. 43 and 44.

Three Estates. Sir David Lindsay. Works. Early English Texts. o. s. 37. Part IV, 3.

Three Ladies of London. R. Wilson. Hazlitt's Dodsley. Vol. VI.

Three Lords and Three Ladies of London. R. Wilson. Hazlitt's Dodsley. Vol. VI.

Tide Tarrieth No Man. George Wapull. Jahrbuch der deutschen Shakespeare Gesellschaft. Vol. XLIII.

Trial of Treasure. *** Tudor Facsimile Texts.

Two Lamentable Tragedies. Robert Yarington. Bullen's Old Plays. Vol. IV.

Virtuous Octavia. Samuel Brandon. Malone Society Reprints.

Warning for Fair Women. *** Simpson's School of Shakespeare. Vol. II. New York, 1878.

Wars of Cyrus. *** Tudor Facsimile Texts.

Wealth and Health. *** Malone Society Reprints.

White Devil. John Webster. Mermaid edition. ed. by J. A. Symonds.

Wisdom of Doctor Doddipoll. *** Tudor Facsimile Texts.

Woman Killed with Kindness. Thomas Heywood. ed. by Katherine L. Bates. Boston, 1917. (Belles Lettres.)

Yorkshire Tragedy. *** Shakespeare Apocrypha.